AF290965

RINASCIMENTO

RINASCIMENTO

The Story of SSC Napoli's Historic 2022/23
Serie A Victory Under Luciano Spalletti

TOM UNDERHILL

First published by Pitch Publishing, 2024

Pitch Publishing
9 Donnington Park,
85 Birdham Road,
Chichester, West Sussex,
PO20 7AJ
www.pitchpublishing.co.uk
info@pitchpublishing.co.uk

A CIP catalogue record is available for this book
from the British Library.

ISBN 978 1 80150 699 1

Printed and bound in the UK on FSC® certified paper in line
with our continuing commitment to ethical business practices,
sustainability and the environment.

Typesetting and origination by Pitch Publishing

Printed and bound by CPI Anthony Rowe, UK

Contents

Acknowledgements

AS NEWS filtered in of Rudi Garcia's firing from Napoli, I was not in my usual surroundings. Rather than being at a desk and formulating my thoughts and notes on the matter for the purpose of this book, I was sitting on a beach in Nha Trang, Vietnam. Most of the beaches we had sat on during our eight-week trip across Thailand, Cambodia and Vietnam were breathtaking in their views and tranquillity. This one was different, with a darker grain of sand and swirling black clouds conjuring hazardous sea conditions. In truth, as I read about the situation in Naples, it was the first time I had thought about Napoli or even football in the best part of six weeks.

As a football obsessive, I had been certain that there would be ways to keep in touch with the game whilst away. Bars would show matches, I would be able to watch the early kick-offs just after dinner time, and there was always the internet and social media to keep me updated. And yet, happily, I failed to do most of these things. Scores were missed, barely a second of action watched, and phones were kept firmly in pockets. There are times where football can feel like the most important thing in the world. Even Carlo Ancelotti once said that 'football is the most important of the least important things'. The passion of those that follow it, the history of everything that has gone before and now the sums of money invested mean that football has become an all-consuming lifestyle that can absorb you into its orbit. I won't be alone in succumbing to it. My love of football grew into a writing passion, then a research subject and then latterly a job. There comes a point where it becomes too much.

Those eight weeks in South East Asia will remain a cherished memory for all my life. The change in routine and food and way of living shook us from the everyday mundanities of life in the United Kingdom and nourished us in every sense. Months later, I still find myself scrolling through photographs late at night. There was no yearning for football, or a sense that I was being left behind by its rolling news cycle. It continued to exist in the same way that I was continuing to exist 8,000 miles away.

Returning to England meant a need to continue my work on this book. Time away from football had ignited new enthusiasm for the story I was telling, and the events in Italy during that time had added new flavour to the story. Rather than ending the book on the high of Napoli lifting the Serie A trophy into the sky, a season of alarming contrast followed it to demonstrate how fickle and finite football can be. Luciano Spalletti was gone, Victor Osimhen had furiously demanded to leave the club, Khvicha Kvaratskhelia had regressed in form and Napoli had slumped down the league table in one of the worst defences of a Serie A title in history. Not only was the previous season's success remarkable by itself; it was now framed against the chaos that followed.

That time away from the game and writing also changed the way I wanted to approach the book. Tactical and systemic patterns on the pitch had long been my niche within my writing, all supported by numbers and data to elevate conclusions through statistical evidence. Perhaps it was the environment I had been in for two months before, but there was a new type of story I wanted to tell about redemption and reaching nirvana. There existed this perfect symmetry between Luciano Spalletti and Napoli. Two respected and admired factors in Italian football that were still reaching for the ultimate prize. Their legacies depended on it. If winning Serie A was what they yearned for most, each would not be the other's first choice to secure that dream. Both had shown an inability to haul themselves over the line and ruthlessly grab titles. Both had been hurt by painful experience and having their names disparaged by influential characters. The perennial bridesmaids of Italian football found each other and found their calling.

This is a long and rambling way of saying that without taking time away from football, spending time with my partner Paige, and rethinking what I wanted to see in football, this book might have turned out very differently. As a result, it is only an improved product and one that I am proud of.

In no particular order, thank you to the following people for lending their time and thoughts to the creation of this book: Patrick Kendrick, Mikha Gabechava, Joe Fischetti, Mattia Montanaro, Kaustubh Pandey, Francesco Sani, Conor Clancy and Ben Bocsak.

Paige, the most wonderful person I have ever met. Luckily that meeting came nearly eight years ago and I have had the privilege to be with you and live with you ever since. Nothing would be possible without having you in my corner and supporting me like you do. I love you more than you will ever know.

My mum and dad, inspirational and kind beyond measure. My brother Toby, the funniest and smartest person I know and one I am so proud of. To Aid, Liv, Fin and Dic, my best friends who have never doubted me or stopped believing in what I am doing. Neil and Mand, my parents-in-law who have always been there and made me feel so at home. All my grandparents, family, friends and work colleagues. I thank all of you so, so much.

The final person to address is my grandad, Bill (or Bubba as we called him). I submitted my pitch for this book little more than a week after he passed away in January 2023. I miss him terribly, and will never forget calling him to tell him I had had my first book proposal accepted back in March 2021. The most interested and open-minded person I could ever meet. Always with a book in his hand and an interesting perspective on matters, always with a youthful interest in the world and willing to look at things in a new way. I could not have had a greater role model, nor one to forever mark myself against as a person.

This book is for you, Bubba.

Introduction

'Many besought the aid of the gods, but still more imagined there were no gods left, and that the universe was plunged into eternal darkness for evermore.'

PLINY THE Younger was a Roman poet and philosopher, whose letters and musings were published in nearly 20 volumes across his life and after his death. Regarded as one of the great thinkers of his time, the work that defined the younger Pliny's life was one born of circumstance and total coincidence. Living in a villa across the Bay of Naples from Naples itself, Pliny the Younger recorded a first-hand account of the eruption of Mount Vesuvius in AD 79. It is the only one of its kind, and stands alongside the eternally encased remains of those that tried to escape the lethal flow of ash and magma as the most reputable source on the event.

In his letters, Pliny described the cloud rising from an unidentified mountain top, watching on from a road leading into Pompeii. Each plume of smoke was 'blotched and dirty, according to the amount of soil and ashes it carried with it'. The letters were sent to Tacitus, a Roman historian who sought to research and tell the events of the disaster, but also of the rescue mission. Pliny's uncle, Pliny the Elder, was a naval commander (as well as an author and environmental commentator) and was stationed in Misenum (now Miseno) directly across the Bay of Naples from Pompeii. Upon the alarm being sounded, Pliny the Elder had set sail across the bay with a fleet. Whether this was in fact a rescue attempt, or a journey of curiosity for one of the empire's most inquisitive ecological minds, remains to be seen. What is certain is that Pliny the Elder had died on board his ship before reaching Pompeii. Many speculate that it was asphyxiation caused by the toxic fumes of the eruption; others say cardiac arrest afflicted him.

The news of his death was the main matter of concern for Tacitus, but Pliny's then-18-year-old nephew went beyond accounting for his uncle's passing. His accounts were detailed and clear, describing the wailing and cries heard from Pompeii as the terrible concoction billowed from Vesuvius' peak and trapped its residents. The quote at the top of page 11 painted explicitly the desperation of those fleeing. Only blind faith could guide these people to safety.

Such bleak and miserable circumstances can hardly be applied to any other. Life-taking volcanic eruptions are rare, and few can ever be classified to have caused death on such a wide scale as Vesuvius' nearly two millennia ago. However, that pleading with a greater entity to be the saviour is an act not so unaccustomed to Neapolitans in far more recent history.

Often treated as the black sheep of Italy, far south of the country's richest cities in the north, Naples has often waged a battle for acceptance. Whether it is the status of being an outcast, of being neglected, or even curated by the very geography upon which they stand, there is a defiance and bite to being Neapolitan. Southern Italy's searing heat and its position beneath an active volcano, combined with an unemployment rate that has at times been double the national average, and a reputation for housing organised crime, can do that to a city.

Once in a generation, Naples' prayers for a divine moment of transcendent inspiration for itself and its people are answered. It might not be in the way those that befell Vesuvius had hoped for, but the 20th century produced a figure elevated above that of a human by the city itself. Diego Armando Maradona's arrival in Naples in 1984 promised to answer the city's prayers. Despite being Italy's third-largest city (963,000, with a wider population of 3.1 million in 2022), Naples had played a limited role in the development of Italy's favourite pastime: football. Rome, Milan, Turin and Florence had dominated the sport's growth, tapping into rich surrounding catchment areas to produce talented players that could win their respective cities titles and championships. With the exception of two Coppa Italia triumphs in 1961/62 and 1975/76, the Napoli trophy cabinet was bare domestically.

Maradona's arrival changed everything. One of the world's best players became one of history's iconic sportsmen during his stay in Naples, and with it elevated the city's standing within Italy and even Europe. Such glow fades with time, and over 30 years on from the Argentine's departure, Naples cried out once more for a new phenomenon.

The spectre of Maradona still dances across the pitch at the Stadio San Paolo; the stadium that in 2020 was renamed after its greatest-ever player. Every coach and player to don the capital 'N' on their chest is reminded of the pressure of wearing that shirt. Maradona's shirt. Some have thrived under its weight while some have buckled. It has been over 30 years since he played his last match in Naples, and until 2023 was the last Napoli captain to hoist the Serie A trophy aloft. Barren times followed, with the indelible sense of loss that their beloved son was no longer playing for their club coupled with struggling performances on the pitch and financial ruin off it. Some would be forgiven for thinking that football in Naples started and ended with Diego Maradona.

In the three decades following Maradona's departure, Napoli sank as low as is possible before rising and competing again. Financial power elevated the club towards the top of Italian football once again, even if they no longer had the superpowers of a Maradona in their team. Three Coppa Italia trophies between 2011 and 2020 were nothing to be sneered at and to most clubs outside of Italy's north this would have been an impressive feat. The football was, at times, electrifying. Maurizio Sarri, a coach with a throwback image and attitude, developed a side to compete with a great modern Juventus team that won admiration across the continent for its originality and commitment to attacking football. However, even Sarri left Naples without a league title. They came desperately close, but Sarri left to join Chelsea, where he would win the first top-flight silverware of his career. In many respects, Sarri was the modern metaphor for Napoli in the same way that Maradona had been for the whole city in the late 1980s. Sarri was forced to overcome preconceptions of his style and suitability for the role of coach at such a giant club. He had coached part-time in the lower divisions as recently as 2005, standing on the touchline with a cigarette balanced on his bottom lip and building his way up to reach Napoli and take them to the brink of a third Serie A title. Beautiful, winning football masterminded by a doubted and grizzled underdog.

Napoli was fighting a lone battle against the power of the northern region as every Serie A title between 2001 and 2022 was won by a side from either Milan or Turin. This power shift mimicked the politics of Italian society. Naples had long been sneered at and looked down on by the richer northern states and cities. High poverty rates and a sizeable community of Travellers made the city an easy subject for derision and discrimination and helped to harvest a bullish fighting spirit that runs through its people. But how long can a club that size with a history as storied and prominent within football culture deem itself an underdog?

The irony is that it took a coach as frustrated as the club to win that treasured third Scudetto. Much like Napoli, Luciano Spalletti had won respect and admiration for his philosophy and coaching career without being Serie A champion. He had come close in two spells at Roma, whereby the first saw him pipped by the era's mighty Inter side and a club-record points tally in the second was still not enough to overthrow the next decade's greatest side, Juventus. Spalletti had been a footnote in Italian football's 21st century, a 'do you remember?' anecdote that could be applied to his impish Udinese side, his mould-breaking Roma, his initially successful spell in Russia with Zenit St Petersburg and then his stabilising role at Inter. Opinion divided wherever he travelled. The football was always exquisite, built upon ideals of heavy possession and choking the opposition deep before snapping quickly through the gears, as well as an aggressive press that snatched the ball back right after losing it. Fans warmed to his charming manner and beautiful meandering metaphors and quotes, before growing wearied when the clubs he operated at turned on him or pulled the rug from beneath his feet. For the football purist, Spalletti was a coach you loved to watch. For the fan of Spalletti's clubs, that only took you so far before questions of his mental capacity to win the biggest matches and claim titles became loud and overbearing. As of the start of the 2022/23 season, Luciano Spalletti was into his fourth decade in management and had still not won Serie A.

This is the story of two wandering souls colliding to change each other's existence forever. Luciano Spalletti and Napoli were not destined to meet. One imagines that, had their respective experiences been more successful in the year preceding their partnership, they might not have found each other at all. Spalletti had spent two decades as a Serie A coach competing against Napoli and testing each coach's tactical wits without ever knowing that they would be the club to offer him his renaissance. His and Napoli's *rinascimento*.

The stature and relevance of both Spalletti and Napoli were deserving of a Scudetto. There is only so much comfort to be taken from being reminisced about as a 'nearly', or one that you had to be there to enjoy. 'Remember when Spalletti converted Francesco Totti into a false nine? What a team!' or 'How amazing were Maurizio Sarri's Napoli? What a shame they didn't win a title.' Stories such as those get lost to the sands of time when stood alongside the physical presence of a trophy. True Serie A fans would acknowledge that worse coaches than Spalletti, and weaker teams than Napoli in the mid to late 2010s won Serie A titles. It counted for very little until that sweet moment of release at the end of the 2022/23 season.

This is a football book, but also one about personal endeavour. Of a man trusting his ability even after decades of being doubted and questioned. Of a club that still clung to glory days that were 30 years behind and yet felt within touching distance of replicating those halcyon days. *Rinascimento* is about emotion, and the explosion of joy that comes when a long-awaited moment eventually comes to pass. How do you celebrate it accordingly? Is there any precedent for how to act or how to feel? Will the pressure and build-up be so intense and anticipated that nothing could truly reflect the magnitude of it? Perhaps pertinently, where do we go from here?

From Naples Foot-Ball Club to Napoli Soccer: A brief history of SSC Napoli

NAPOLI'S HISTORY can be divided into three very distinct eras: the formative years, the Maradona years, and the bankruptcy and post-bankruptcy era.

Beginning with the formative years, the club formed in its original guise in 1905 with the amalgamation of two Neapolitan football sides: Football Club Partenopeo and Naples Foot-Ball and Cricket Club. This was at a time of significant British involvement in Italian football as workers migrated to Italy and spread the rules of association football. Two famous examples are Genoa who claim to be the oldest club in Italy thanks to their formation under James Richardson Spensley in 1897 (the club had already existed as part of a wider football, athletics and cricket club formed in 1893), and Herbert Kilpin's founding of AC Milan (to be referred to as Milan from hereon) in 1899. Naples' significance as a port and dockyard encouraged English maritime workers to relocate there, and this is how William Poths and Italian engineer Amedeo Salsi came to create Naples Foot-Ball and Cricket Club.

Naples hosted a number of football and athletic clubs at the time, but it was Naples Foot-Ball Club that quickly rose to the fore as the most powerful and prolific in the city. One year after formation, Naples became the first side from central-southern Italy to join the *Federazione Italiana del Football* (known as the FIF, Italian football's original governing body) but were hamstrung by the distances required to travel in order to compete with the northern teams. This forced Naples to withdraw from the competition before they had competed, and wait until other sides from Campania would also play. Eventually the issue was forced by two Neapolitan clubs (including Naples) asking the FIF to create another tier of the competition that would be specific to Campanian teams, and so the Terza Categoria Campania was formed. Back-to-back titles took Naples up to the second tier of Italian football, and the club would win that title two years running too.

A problem emerged in 1911 when the international players broke away to form a new Naples-based club called Unione Sportiva Internazionale Napoli. This was not uncommon, with a better-known example being in Milan in 1908 when a disagreement in the AC Milan board over signing international players caused Swiss and certain Italian members to split and form Foot-Ball Club Internazionale (Inter Milan, or Inter). The two Neapolitan clubs competed ferociously over the coming years and a power struggle developed between them. Both survived World War I and would eventually merge in 1922 to ease the post-war financial pressure that had mounted upon them. Naples was united with one main football team under the name Foot-Ball Club Internazionale-Naples.

This mashing together of names was shortened to FBC Internaples colloquially, then AC Napoli, and then Napoli.

A short number of years later, with the kit already a combination of Naples' light blue shirt with Internazionale's white shorts, the bold 'N' of the Internazionale badge appeared on the club shirt. The white 'N' on the light blue circle became one of European's football's most iconic club badges. Its simplicity and boldness make it instantly recognisable to the eye. 'N' means Napoli, and nothing else. The two original clubs had competed in the southern division of the Prima Divisione (top flight), and a run to the Lega Sud Final in 1925/26 secured Internaples a spot in the Divisione Nazionale for the start of the next season. The FIF had become the FIGC (*Federazione Italiana Giuoco Calcio*) and the fascist government under Benito Mussolini had desires for Italy's top football competition to be fully national, and not split into regional groups as it had been. Competing in a new competition also saw another name change as Internaples became 'Associazione Calcio Napoli', and the turn of the 1930s also saw the reintroduction of English influence on the club for the first time since William Poths' involvement.

William Garbutt is regarded as one of the founding fathers of Italian football, having moved to Genoa after a playing career in England and coaching the club for 15 years. Garbutt was an early tactician who sought to raise the game in Italy to the levels of those in England and left Genoa in 1927 having won three domestic titles to become Italy's national coach and then the first-ever manager of AS Roma. Napoli were next on his tour of influence, and under Garbutt they finished third twice between 1932 and 1934.

Garbutt left Naples and Italy in 1935 for Spain, where he would win the league with Athletic Bilbao before returning to coach Milan and then two further stints with Genoa. The first of his latter two stints with Genoa was marred by the influence of Mussolini's regime, which imprisoned and then exiled Garbutt for being a non-national. Like Genoa and Roma, Napoli's early years saw their brightest moments come under the coaching of William Garbutt. Those two third-place finishes were the highest they would finish in Serie A for 30 years as he influenced the Italian game wherever he went. The common title of 'Mister' that Italian players and fans use to address their manager can be traced back to Garbutt; the first 'Mister' of Italian football.

Garbutt was arguably the second-most important figure in Napoli's recent history at that point. The honour of first place could be awarded to Attila Sallustro, a Paraguay-born forward who had moved to Naples as a child and rose through the ranks of both Internazionale Napoli and Internaples. Sallustro played for the club at senior level for 12 years (as well as a year before the merger and five years as a youth player). He became known as *Il Divino* ('The Divine') and was beloved for not only being a superb striker, but also not asking for a wage from the club. They did reward him with gifts such as a Fiat motor car, but Sallustro had come from a wealthy family and chose not to take financial payment. In Garbutt and Sallustro, Napoli had two superstars to transform their side, along with Croatia-born Italian attacker Antonio Vojak.

The second third-place finish, in 1933/34, qualified Napoli for the European Cup and their first taste of European competition. That would turn out to be

Garbutt's last season in Naples and the start of a decline at the club. Many of the supporting cast behind Sallustro were sold and the great man's form suffered as a result. Many even correlated his deteriorating performances with his marriage to Russian actress Lucy D'Albert. After over 250 appearances and 107 goals for Napoli, Sallustro was sold to Salernitana in 1937 to close Napoli's greatest early chapter. He remained the club's record goalscorer for five decades until the arrival of another supremely talented South American in Naples in the 1980s. Sallustro would return to the city to live until his death in 1983, becoming Napoli coach in 1961 and working as the director of the club's stadium between 1960 and 1981.

This decline had coincided with the new ownership of Achille Lauro, a local businessman and politician who had been born into the wealth of a ship-owning family and had risen to political prominence as a member of the fascist party under Mussolini. Napoli's finances were dwindling, so Lauro sold many of their best players (including Sallustro) and as a result recorded lower Serie A finishes of tenth, seventh and 14th before the turn of the 1940s. In 1939/40, Napoli finished one place above relegated Liguria and were spared relegation by their superior goal difference. The nightmare of relegation that had seemed inevitable came to pass in 1942 and Napoli would remain in Serie B until after World War II when a restructuring of the league system allowed the club to return to Serie A, despite finishing third and one place outside of the promotion places in the most recently played season (1942/43).

The decades that followed the war saw Napoli bounce between Serie A and B without troubling the very pinnacle of the top flight. Relegations marked this era as the club failed to truly establish itself as a Serie A mainstay, although they did feature in the first ever live match broadcast on Italian television in 1956. Another notable moment within this period was Napoli's move to Stadio San Paolo in Fuorigrotta in 1959 following an 11-year construction period. It was known initially as Stadio del Sole before being renamed in 1963 to honour Saint Paul the Apostle, and at the time held up to 100,000 spectators. Its first match as Napoli's official home venue saw Juventus beaten 2-1 in front of an enormous crowd.

As a stadium, the brutalist Stadio San Paolo is as intimidating and sprawling as one could ever find. Rather than building vertically and stacking spectators upon each other, it staggers outwards to hold those in attendance at a milder angle. A running track wraps itself around the playing surface to keep fans even further from the pitch, and whilst many Italian stadia of the time had this feature, it remains in place at Napoli. Then there's the structure itself. A mass of planted concrete struts burst from the ground to hold the weight of this giant, hollowed disc. Between the fans and the running track lies a deep concrete moat, sunk beneath the level of the pitch and so low that those within it crane their necks upwards to look at the bouncing fans above. Smoke billows out and flags fly over the moat in an atmosphere as close to a gladiator's entrance as one can picture.

A first Coppa Italia came in 1962, just one year after relegation, and their first piece of top level silverware in the same season that they were promoted back to Serie A. This made Napoli the first side to win the competition whilst competing in the second tier. Napoli also changed their name to Società Sportiva Calcio Napoli, becoming the SSC Napoli that they are today. This would not be the final time their name would change, however.

Unfortunately, this bright moment was followed by another relegation: their second in three years and fourth since the formation of Serie A after the end of World War II. Napoli's return to Serie A came in 1965/66 and started a prolonged period of stability without dropping down a division. More than just stabilising, Napoli rose to become one of Italy's prominent sides under manager Bruno Pesaola. The Argentine coach had made over 240 appearances for Napoli as a player and had moved seamlessly into a coaching career at just 37. Napoli was Pesaola's first job in management and he delivered the club that precious Coppa Italia trophy in his first season. From there, the Argentine oversaw Napoli's rise and development, with the pinnacle coming in 1967/68 with an impressive second-place finish in Serie A. That team featured the attacking talent of José Altafini, a Brazilian-born striker who had appeared at international level for both Brazil and Italy and had been a star at Milan between 1958 and 1965.

Another notable name was that of Dino Zoff, a 25-year-old goalkeeper who had joined from Mantova at the start of that season. Zoff's career would take him to the heights of European Championship winner in 1968 and then, 14 years later, World Cup champion at 42. Zoff and Altafini were the stars of Napoli's greatest side since the days of Sallustro and Vojak under William Garbutt, a side that could compete in cup competitions and maintain a high level throughout the rigours of the league campaign. Pesaola departed in 1968 and his credentials as a coach were proven by winning Serie A in his first season with Fiorentina. He would return to Napoli twice more, firstly in 1976 for one solitary season and then again in 1982 for one more. Not only had Pesaola created a competitive Napoli side, he also continued a rich heritage of Argentinian association with Napoli that would flow right through to the present day.

Unlike when Garbutt's departure sparked a decline, Napoli continued their progress post-Pesaola. Two spells under manager Giuseppe Chiappella returned positive results including a third-place finish in 1970/71. However, it was under the coaching of Brazilian Luís Vinício that Napoli made their greatest strides. Between 1973 and 1976, Napoli came third, second and fifth in Serie A as well as winning the Coppa Italia in 1975/76. This success and development can be attributed to stability in the boardroom. Napoli had had seven different presidents since 1960, with no one figure remaining in position for longer than three years in that time. Corrado Ferlaino had already had a go at running the club between 1969 and 1971, and returned in 1972 to embark on a prolonged period as president.

The star of that Napoli team was Sergio Clerici, who, despite arriving as a 32-year-old in 1973 and plying his trade at five different Italian clubs prior, caught fire in Naples. He scored 14 goals in their second-place finish in 1974/75 having scored 17 the season before. That period, which could claim to be the greatest in Napoli's history up to that point, featured a return to European competition via the 1974/75 UEFA Cup, an Anglo-Italian League Cup success in 1976 and an impressive run in the European Cup Winners' Cup to reach the semi-finals in 1976/77.

Napoli rolled on as Ferlaino's presidential spell ended briefly in 1983 only to resume that same year until 1993. Ferlaino had gradually increased his involvement in the club from his initial minority share bought in 1967. His financial stake had risen in the late 1960s to a point where he became majority shareholder as well as being elected president in 1969. His control of the club was total, and the results on the pitch proved his value. Under Ferlaino's stewardship, Napoli were not relegated once between 1969 and 1993, having had three relegations in the decade before he became involved at the club.

His greatest success was still to come as the 1980s turned Napoli into a household name across the globe.

Throughout his life, Diego Maradona rarely found himself at peace with his surroundings. The social pressures of being treated like a god amongst men whilst also displaying the same frailties and flaws that mankind does engulfed him. Even when he was at his brilliant best as a footballer, speculation and interrogation followed his every move off the pitch. However, Maradona did not always help himself in this regard, and gave the baying hordes plenty of ammunition to play with. The contrast between his genius with a ball and troubled personal life made Naples the perfect home for him: unconventional, raw, emotional, beautiful and not to everyone's taste. But how did the greatest player in the world come to Napoli?

Maradona had not yet blossomed into the world's greatest. He had endured a wretched two-year spell in

Barcelona where injury curtailed his potential and he struggled to show the best of himself. Perhaps the image most associated with Maradona's time at Camp Nou was his ridiculous flying kick that caused him to be sent off against Athletic Bilbao in the 1984 Copa del Rey Final having spent months out with a bad injury. It perfectly summarised the frustrations of a troubled mind. He never played for Barcelona again, and was sold to Napoli for the equivalent of €12 million. With Italy's premier sides already containing top talents in Maradona's position, Napoli acted on the opportunity by offering a financially struggling star significant wages and the opportunity to be the patron saint of an aspiring side; one that had finished 12th the season before.

The deal would prove to have consequences further down the line, but as Maradona rose from the depths of Stadio San Paolo to an hysterical reception, that felt unimportant. A star had arrived, and Napoli could dream. Neapolitans were so desperate for Maradona to join that there were instances of fans chaining themselves to Stadio San Paolo and others going on hunger strike in an effort to pressure the transfer into being confirmed.

There was another layer to the connection. Maradona's origins in the rough barrios of Buenos Aires bore similarities to the city he was moving to: a rough and hardy edge that many would not wish to experience, yet beneath it was a community and spirit that connected its people despite their circumstances. On his unveiling as a Napoli player, Maradona said: 'I want to become the idol of the poor children of Naples because they are like I was when I lived in Buenos Aires.'

The Maradona effect was not felt immediately, although the Argentine's talents were evident quickly as he top-scored for the club with 17 goals. An eighth-place finish did not scream of a team reborn, but Napoli lost just one of their last 17 matches as Maradona gelled with his new team-mates and transformed their domestic form. Crucially, Maradona was fit and available: no Napoli player made more appearances than his 30 that season. Concerns over whether Napoli had invested in a physically declining superstar eased and demonstrated the benefits of a happy and healthy mental state on the body itself.

1985/86 saw further improvement as Napoli climbed to third place, albeit losing eight times and not reaching the heights of winners Juventus, who themselves were propelled by the creative attacking talents of a genius playmaker: Michel Platini. Napoli inflicted one of Juventus' three defeats that season, a 1-0 win in Naples with Maradona scoring a stunning chipped free kick for the match's only goal. Napoli also beat Inter and Milan with *I Rossoneri* defeated on their own turf at San Siro as Napoli began to punch up in the manner they had always wanted. The established giants of the north would always hold the heritage and prestige of Italian football, but Napoli were the aggressors, bloodying noses of the elite. That season had also seen the arrival of Ottavio Bianchi as head coach, having secured newly promoted Como's Serie A status the season before. Napoli were looking up, dragged towards the glass ceiling by Maradona's magic and supported by a hard-working and committed supporting cast.

Maradona's own glass ceiling was smashed that very summer in Mexico when he lifted the World Cup trophy with Argentina. His performances were of a mind-blowing standard, tearing whole teams apart by himself and leaving them in his wake. One of football's iconic images is Maradona hoisted on the shoulders of his team-mates at the Azteca Stadium. It confirmed him as the greatest talent in world football; one that Napoli were proud to call their own. The World Cup was still not enough for Maradona. Rather than feel quenched by the glory of winning the game's greatest prize, he set about using his wizardry to propel Napoli forwards.

Finishing third entered Napoli into the UEFA Cup for 1986/87; however, that novelty was quickly forgotten after losing to Toulouse in the first round. The real magic occurred in the league where Napoli lost just one of their first 19 in the 30-match Serie A season. The highlight of this run was a 3-1 away win over Juventus that cemented their place at the top of the table for a third week. It was a symbolic victory in coming from behind to beat the defending champions with three late goals, and from that point Napoli never looked back. They remained top until the season ended even when momentum began to slow as they won just three of their last 11 matches. Juventus could not catch them however, and a first Scudetto was Napoli's. Over 80 years since the first building blocks were laid, Napoli were champions of Italy for the first time. Fans flooded the field as other results confirmed the championship on the penultimate weekend of the season and a scrum formed around Maradona as he embraced his team-mates. The outpouring of emotion matched that in the stands, where blue smoke billowed and men wept.

The first Serie A title for Napoli was also the first ever by a team from the south, and it was celebrated as such: a triumph over the judging and condescending north who had lorded over the south both in a football sense and in a wider social context. Neapolitans were regarded as un-Italian by many in the north and sneered at for being economically impoverished and even derided for their darker skin colour. Napoli played through cacophonies of whistles and monkey noises every time they travelled north, with many screaming at them to 'Wash!' or be 'cleaned by Vesuvius' fire'. This was Naples' time to hit back at those cruel taunts. Coffins with Juventus flags draped over them were carried through the streets of Naples and effigies and paintings of Maradona appeared on every corner. One year on from winning the World Cup, Maradona was experiencing a sense of adoration and celebration that even Argentina hadn't given him.

'For me, this title means a lot more than winning the World Cup,' he said. 'I won a youth World Cup in Tokyo and I won a World Cup in Mexico last year but on both occasions I was alone. Here, all my family, the city of Naples are with me because I consider myself a son of Naples.'

The 'Son of Naples' wasn't done there. A 4-0 aggregate win over Atalanta in the Coppa Italia Final gave Napoli a domestic double and elevated their success into something even grander. Napoli were domestic dominators, sitting alone at the pinnacle of Italian football with two belts across their torso. For a club and city that had felt so oppressed and undermined for all their existence, this was a surreal feeling. It would be unfair to say that Maradona was merely enabled by the other ten players in that side.

There were many talented and skilled individuals in Napoli's first Scudetto-winning squad, but Maradona was the alien life force that had made dreams come true. Only he could have done that, binding the city to the team by channelling his ability and an acceptance of who he was. An imperfect master.

They nearly followed it up with an almost unthinkable second title in as many years, leading the league for 27 of the 30 matchweeks before crumbling spectacularly to lose four of the final five matches and gift the title to Milan. It was at this time that suggestions of foul play began to grow over Maradona's involvement with the Camorra, a powerful criminal organisation that ran parts of Naples. Maradona's darker side was starting to appear and become more visible as Napoli finished second again in 1988/89 and his not-so-secret cocaine habits and lavish partying tendencies could no longer be covered up. That said, Maradona's performances on the field continued to inspire Napoli to new heights. They won the UEFA Cup in 1988/89, their first major piece of European silverware, featuring a remarkable run to the final in which they beat Juventus and Bayern Munich. The latter of those ties is best known not for the match itself, but Maradona's warm-up. With 'Live is Life' by Opus blaring around the stadium, Maradona spent the duration of the song juggling the ball with ridiculous ease. It went high and then dropped right on to the cushion of his foot before being sent up again, all while having his shoelaces untied and shifting in time with the music. It was poetic in its simplicity.

The scoring burden had been alleviated by the arrival of Brazilian forward Careca in 1987, and the UEFA Cup-winning campaign saw Careca become Napoli's main goal threat by scoring 27 times across all competitions. He and Maradona were as lethal and effective as any attacking connection in Italy, but they were nearly broken apart by a substantial bid from Marseille to try and tempt Maradona away from Naples. The details of the proposed deal were leaked and it fell through, but Napoli punished Maradona for his involvement in the saga and forced him to sit out the first half of the 1989/90 season. His weight fluctuated and the distractions that had previously made him who he was were beginning to frustrate and alienate those around him. The scandals were mounting: cocaine possession, alleged drug trafficking, affairs with multiple women and potentially fathering a son outside of his marriage, refusing to train. All the while, Napoli stormed back to reclaim their Serie A title three years on from last winning it.

This time it felt different. Perhaps it was the novelty and staggering scale of achievement that they had felt three years before, but this success was the beginning of the end for Maradona. That summer, as Italy hosted the 1990 World Cup, Maradona's Argentina met Italy in the semi-finals in Naples. Maradona had publicly implored Neapolitans to reject their nationality and support his Argentina side instead, citing the repression and cruel treatment they had felt by their fellow countrymen. Argentina won, but Maradona reacted furiously as his national anthem was booed at Stadio San Paolo. National newspapers and media outlets that had once protected his image began to turn on him, highlighting every misdemeanour and circling his movements.

It all came to an end in 1991. Maradona was handed a 15-month ban for testing positive for cocaine in a Serie

A match, and he fled Naples under the cover of night. Having arrived to a Beatles-esque reception of screaming hysteria and worship and elevating Naples and Napoli to nirvana, Maradona left in disgrace. He would play for another six years without ever re-finding the magic that he had touched Naples with. His years at Napoli had both blessed and cursed him, the city's darker characteristics equally supporting and destroying him. Maradona and Naples were made for each other, and they did just that. Forever more, Napoli was Maradona.

If the 1980s had been a stunning vista of excellence and silverware for Napoli, the 1990s plunged them to the darkest depths. Attempting to find optimism and purpose in the midst of losing an icon such as Diego Maradona would be testing for any club, let alone one so emotional and devoted to the great man as Napoli.

Understandably, Napoli continued to spend lavishly on player recruitment to try and remain relevant in the post-Maradona age. Bright talents appeared, including Gianfranco Zola, Fabio Cannavaro and Benito Carbone, but the financial maintenance required to keep Maradona healthy and happy had burned a deep hole in Napoli's pockets. *These Football Times* wrote that the deal to bring Maradona to Naples in 1984 had only been possible as a result of a local politician exercising his connections with the banks to obtain a sizeable loan.

Maradona's successes on the pitch had been vast and varied, but the picture off the pitch was far from healthy. President Ferlaino's tenure ended in 1993 when he was charged with paying bribes for significant state contracts within his construction business away from the football club. Like Maradona, Ferlaino's unconventional and near-the-knuckle approach to life in Naples had caused issues further down the line. Zola was sold in 1993 and Cannavaro followed two years later as Napoli attempted to balance the books, and their performances suffered. A sixth-place finish in 1993/94 was the club's highest of the decade and Napoli cycled through 16 different head coaches in ten years. Ottavio Bianchi returned midway through a season in 1992 to replace Claudio Ranieri, but even the mastermind behind Napoli's greatest moments of the previous decade could lift them no higher than 11th. Eight years on from their second title under Maradona's captaincy, Napoli were relegated to Serie B for the first time since 1965.

The worst was yet to come. Napoli could not return to Serie A at the first try, finishing ninth and then eventually returning for the 2000/01 season with the top four sides all promoted. It was a short-lived return as they were relegated once again the following season. There would be no sight of Serie A football until 2007 as the dark storm clouds turned even blacker above Naples. Napoli were no longer even competing for promotion. They had sunk so low that they finished 16th in 2002/03 and then 13th in 2003/04, testing the bottom of Serie B rather than the top.

The summer of 2004 witnessed Napoli's darkest day as they were refused a licence to compete in Serie B, having accumulated estimated debts of €70 million. The National Associated Press Agency (ANSA, standing for Agenzia Nazionale Stampa Associata) declared Napoli bankrupt in August 2004. The club was put up for auction, and a bid of €37 million was accepted to buy the club's remains after they were put into administration.

That bid had been submitted by Italian film mogul Aurelio De Laurentiis. The then-55-year-old producer had established himself as one of Italian film's most important figures in connecting the non-Italian world to its movies. He had been introduced to the industry by his uncle Dino, who had also been a trailblazer for Italian film, and Aurelio's father had founded the Filmauro media company in 1975. Aurelio assumed control of the company, and also became a member of the National Italian American Foundation and had been president of the International Federation of Film Producers Associations between 1993 and 2003. Crucially, De Laurentiis' father had been born in the Neapolitan commune of Torre Annunziata, and whilst Aurelio was born in Rome and had no affiliation to football, he claimed to have been taken as a child by his father to watch Napoli in the 1950s. By his own admission, De Laurentiis did not know the rules of football upon buying the club in 2004. The man behind the company that produced the *Hannibal Lecter* film series would soon take on the starring role of his own story as chairman and president of the newly formed Napoli Soccer. He had even tried to buy the club in 1999 for €102 million only to see his bid rejected. 'I put €37 million on the table just to buy a piece of paper, and we started a new adventure.'

The bankruptcy had forced the club to change their name, although the iconic 'N' was retained on the crest of the light blue shirts. The terms of the bankruptcy also required Napoli to restart as a Serie C1 side, meaning they would compete in the third division for the first time since the restructuring of the Italian football system post-World War II.

Naturally, the first objective for Napoli Soccer was to scale the leagues. Any hopes of re-establishing themselves as a functioning and successful club would only be tenable if they were back in Serie A, and whilst they failed to gain promotion to Serie B in their first season, they gathered impressive home support with attendances regularly hitting 50,000 despite being in the third tier. De Laurentiis' model was to acquire highly talented young players and develop them into saleable assets to improve the club's financial position.

There was a ruthlessness to De Laurentiis' operation, one that would remain evident right through to the current day as his first coach, Gian Piero Ventura, was fired in January 2005 and replaced by Edoardo Reja. 'Edy' Reja was a seasoned head coach, having worked across all tiers of Italian football for over two decades. Reja made Napoli immediately competitive even if they missed out on promotion by three points. The team's main issue was a lack of goals, scoring just 45 times in 34 league matches with their top scorer (Roberto Sosa) hitting the back of the net eight times.

This all changed in 2005/06, when Napoli put their disappointment of the previous season behind them to romp to the Serie C1 title by 13 points. They remained relatively goal shy and added just three goals to their tally of a year prior, but their rock-solid defence conceded a mere 20 goals across the campaign. This was and remains a staple of Reja's teams; a resolute and strong defence that first and foremost prevents his sides losing. It is why he became such a trusted pair of hands for Serie A sides facing relegation and needing a coach to pull them back from the brink.

Perhaps more importantly, even than promotion, was Napoli Soccer were renamed. After two years without their original name, the club was officially renamed as Società Sportiva Calcio Napoli. SSC Napoli were back.

Reja's work was not done. Napoli went up again in 2006/07, making it back-to-back promotions under his management. This season coincided with Juventus' relegation into Serie B as a result of the *Calciopoli* scandal; a traumatising event in Italian football history that uncovered a systemic approach to pressuring referees into influencing matches. Juve were at the heart of the story and were stripped of two Serie A titles as well as being demoted. This all meant that the division was as tough as Napoli could have imagined for their re-entry.

Naturally, Juventus' squad was far superior to any in the league and they won the title and promotion at the very first time of asking. Napoli finished second, with their defence the tightest of any side (29 goals conceded), and their attack functional if not inspiring (52 goals scored was lower than five of the top seven). Of those 52 goals, Emanuele Calaiò scored 14, having also scored 18 in Serie C1 in 2005/06. Calaiò had played at youth level for Italy's national team from under-15 right through to under-21 and had impressed at Pescara in his early 20s. Napoli signed him as a 23-year-old, and Calaiò had repaid them by leading their attack for both of their successive promotion seasons. Calaiò was a case study for how De Laurentiis wanted his recruitment to work; sign young and sell high. 'We bought Calaiò while he was at Pescara, you will see what he will be worth in a season,' warned De Laurentiis in November 2006. He was right, although Calaiò's hot streak was interrupted as Napoli returned to Serie A and De Laurentiis' purse strings loosened to attract non-Italian talents to ensure Napoli would not be seen in Serie B again.

The summer of 2007 saw the arrivals of four overseas talents that would begin to shape Napoli's new era. They were Ezequiel Lavezzi, an energetic Argentine winger; Marcelo Zalayeta, a seasoned Uruguayan striker who had been on Juventus' books for a decade; fellow Uruguayan Walter Gargano; and eye-catching midfielder Marek Hamšik. All four of these arrivals would feature in Napoli's most-used starting 11 in their return to Serie A and collectively the squad's level was raised. Lavezzi quickly established himself as a star in the making. Diminutive, quick-footed and Argentinian, the comparisons to Maradona arrived quickly. His and Hamšik's exploits in front of goal helped Napoli to finish eighth, seven points behind seventh-place Udinese but high enough for a UEFA Cup spot as a result of both that season's Coppa Italia finalists finishing higher than sixth.

In that same 2006 interview, De Laurentiis had spoken boldly of Napoli's ambitions. 'If I say that Napoli must compete with the noblest clubs in the world, I am not exaggerating. We have five or six million fans across the globe, we are a force. We have a duty to compete with Manchester United, Real Madrid, and not just with Juventus, Inter and Milan.' Napoli were still in Serie B at the time, so few could take this seriously. However, as Napoli scaled the tiers of Italian football quickly, and already qualifying for European competition at the first time of asking, De Laurentiis' objective no longer looked so fanciful.

Napoli continued where they left off and lost only two of their opening ten Serie A matches. The curse of the second season, where a team impresses in their first season in a higher division before being found out and brought back to earth the following year, took hold in the autumn and winter of 2008. Seven defeats in nine matches culminated with a 2-0 home loss to Lazio that cost Reja his job as coach. His replacement was Roberto Donadoni, and he too failed to kick Napoli on to the next level in the manner they had hoped. A 12th-place finish was secured but Donadoni won two of the remaining 11 matches of the season with very little improvement shown.

Donadoni continued flattering to deceive in his first full season. He too was fired by De Laurentiis, having won just four of the 18 matches he had presided over in both seasons. Napoli were loitering above the relegation places, and the owner simply could not risk the reputational and financial implications of relegation; he had invested heavily in the summer, including an €18.75 million outlay on striker Fabio Quagliarella. De Laurentiis turned to Walter Mazzarri for his next appointment, a coach who had enjoyed success in guiding Sampdoria to the UEFA Cup a few seasons before. Following the disappointment of Reja's final season and Donadoni's subsequent poor tenure, Mazzarri's hire would prove to be one of the more inspired decisions of De Laurentiis' career. From his appointment in October 2009, Napoli would not lose again in Serie A until February 2010. The football was scintillating as Mazzarri deployed a three-man defence with aggressive wing-backs and allowed creative freedom to his three main weapons, Lavezzi, Quagliarella and

Hamšik. The trio scored a combined 31 goals that season as Mazzarri unlocked their potential, and Napoli soared accordingly. They sat as high as fourth for a long period in the middle of the season only to falter and drop down to sixth by the campaign's end. Mazzarri had turned their fortunes around, having arrived with the side in danger of relegation and ending the season having qualified for the Europa League play-off round.

Walter Mazzarri's first stint (we will return to his second spell much later in the book) was arguably best remembered for the attacking exploits of his front three. They became known as *I Tre Tenori*, meaning 'The Three Tenors', who were an operatic supergroup that included Luciano Pavarotti. Despite his contribution in Mazzarri's first season, Quagliarella was not a member of this famed trio.

He was loaned and eventually sold to Juventus after the season's first match, a Europa League win over two legs against Elfsborg of Sweden. The reason for his sale was the expensive arrival of another South American forward: Edinson Cavani from Palermo for a club-record €17 million. Cavani also bore a nickname; *El Matador* meaning 'The Bullfighter'. The Uruguayan played with a furious intensity and a lethal finish to match, and quickly settled into the front three alongside Lavezzi and Hamšik. In his first season at Napoli, Cavani scored an astonishing 26 Serie A goals, just two behind the league's leading scorer Antonio Di Natale. Cavani scored three hat-tricks, including two in January alone, and made the kind of impact his nickname suggested he might. A special attribute of Cavani's was that he did not require time and space to be impactful, and could make short movements to pull away from a marker and create openings. In a league like Serie A where defenders were physical and sat deep, it was Cavani's intelligence and anticipation that made him so unstoppable.

Mazzari and Cavani propelled Napoli to a third-place finish and Champions League football was secured for the first time since 1990/91. It didn't stop there. Cavani had scored 33 times across all competitions in 2010/11 and matched it the following season. Napoli were poorer in the league than they were a season before, mostly as a result of drawing more matches, but a run to the Champions League quarter-finals made their return to Europe's premier competition worthwhile. The crowning glory of that season, however, was winning the Coppa Italia by beating Juventus 2-0 in the final with Cavani and Hamšik both on the scoresheet with second-half goals. This fourth Coppa Italia in the club's history also marked the first major silverware since De Laurentiis' takeover eight years before. In the grand scheme of his vision, a domestic trophy such as this was small change; however, the level at which Napoli were operating proved that the vision was on track. De Laurentiis wanted Napoli to be competing with the very best. They certainly were now.

One third of *I Tre Tenori* was lost ahead of the 2012/13 season as Ezequiel Lavezzi bid farewell to Naples for the riches of Paris-Saint Germain. Lavezzi had been there since Napoli's first promotion back to Serie A and had become an adored beacon of Napoli's growth. Pizzas and coffees were named after him and the people of Naples felt connected to his impish and maverick style. His replacement would have the unenviable task of not only filling his role in the team but also connecting to the fans. That task fell to Lorenzo Insigne; an even shorter winger who had spent the last two seasons on loan but was a local and lifetime Napoli fan. That season would not see the best of Insigne, but soon even Lavezzi's standing in Naples would be challenged by that of his successor.

Napoli underwhelmed in the Europa League that season having participated in the Champions League a year before, making it through the group stages before crashing out in the first knockout round. On the other hand, their league form hit new heights with a record second-place finish and losing only once at home all season. Just eight matches were spent outside second place throughout the campaign as Napoli began to assert herself as a mainstay at the top of Serie A. Finishing behind the Juventus machine was no shameful feat, and Napoli had now climbed above the Milan clubs to make a claim to be the main contender. They were the top-scoring side in Serie A with 73 goals, and Cavani was crowned *Capocannoniere* (top scorer) for the first time, having scored 29 times in the league.

Cavani had now scored 104 times for the club in just three seasons. To put this in context, the Uruguayan was scoring 0.75 times per match, and only the greats, Maradona and Sallustro, sat ahead of him in the all-time Napoli scoring charts. Cavani was a wanted man, with talk of lucrative transfers away from Italy following his every goal. It turned out to be his last season at Napoli as he followed Lavezzi to the bright lights of Paris for a hefty €64.5 million fee. His star had shone for a short while in Naples, but it would be hard to argue that any player shone brighter than Cavani in the modern era. A long and successful career took him from France to England to Spain and then Argentina, and forever underrated for his role not only as a goalscorer but as a facilitator and tireless worker for his team.

Cavani was not the only departee in 2013. Having extended his contract by just one year the summer before, Walter Mazzarri announced he would be leaving at the end of the 2012/13 season. Speculation had begun to swirl in the build-up to the season's end, and De Laurentiis was vocal in his pressure to reach a conclusion. 'He has four days to decide. When you go you know what you are leaving behind, but you do not know what you will find. The decision is up to him.' De Laurentiis even went on to say: 'The fans shouldn't worry if Cavani or Mazzarri leave, they should only be concerned if De Laurentiis goes!'

Mazzarri did indeed leave and joined Inter. De Laurentiis' response to his most successful coach departing for a rival? 'The Walter Mazzarri years at Napoli are happy ones, but you need two people to make a marriage. But if your wife wants to sleep with someone else, she'll sleep with someone else.' An emphatic way of saying that Mazzarri's head was turned, and De Laurentiis had come to terms with the fact that nothing would make him stay. Even his reasons for appointing Rafael Benítez to replace him continued the metaphor, claiming he liked how 'monogamous' the Spaniard was.

Aside from the managerial position, the money recouped from the Cavani sale had to be used wisely. Rather than trying to spend it all on one like-for-like replacement, which would have been impossible for a striker of Cavani's quality, the squad was bolstered with many new additions. The headline arrival was that of Gonzalo Higuaín from Real Madrid for €37 million. The Argentine came with a burgeoning reputation, having scored over 100 times for Real, and at 25 years old had potential to grow even if he was from a very different mould to Cavani. Higuaín was less mobile than his predecessor and a more classic poaching style of centre-forward. He was one of three signings from Real Madrid in the summer of 2013 as he was joined by José Callejón and Raúl Albiol, and other signings included those of Belgian forward Dries Mertens from PSV Eindhoven and goalkeeper Pepe Reina from Liverpool as De Laurentiis flexed his financial muscle. With both Milan clubs in turmoil, there was a realistic opportunity for Napoli to become the second-best side in Italy behind Juventus with the view of pushing their bitter rival all the way across all competitions.

The new-look attacking trio of Higuaín, Callejón and Mertens, with Lorenzo Insigne rotating in and out, was not yet at the level of 'The Three Tenors', but between them they posted 46 goals in the 2013/14 Serie A season. Benítez threw out Mazzarri's 3-4-3 formation and adopted a robust and stable 4-2-3-1 that was defensively sound but also allowed one more attacking player to feature. They scored more goals in Benítez's debut season (79) than they had in any campaign under Mazzarri as the goals were distributed across the forwards. Napoli never once dropped out of the top three during the entire campaign and qualified for the Champions League for a second year running. Their foray into the Champions League that season was also promising as they won four of their six matches, only to be knocked out by Arsenal's superior goal difference. A round of 16 elimination in the Europa League was a disappointment, but Benítez's superb debut campaign in Naples was rewarded with the Coppa Italia trophy, a second title in three years for the club. The initial two-year contract awarded to the coach was beginning to seem overly cautious, and an extension was seen as a foregone conclusion.

De Laurentiis wanted more. Two Coppa Italias in three years was an impressive feat for a club that had been in Serie B less than a decade before. His financial outlay had allowed Napoli to maintain their level towards the top end of the table even when selling their best players. It was undeniable that the president would grow tired of winning cups at the expense of securing that first league title since the days of Maradona. So whilst Napoli added another trophy to their cabinet the following season, the Supercoppa Italiana, finishing fifth and 14 points behind their 2013/14 tally represented a step back. In the spring of 2015, De Laurentiis began to vent to the press. 'I have spent €386 million on the purchase of players and I demand commitment. I dislike the idea of a training camp as part of the club's philosophy but Naples is a city full of distractions.'

This would not be the last time that De Laurentiis would threaten his squad with the proverbial stick of a training camp. Napoli undeniably regressed in that second season under Benítez, and squandered the opportunity of making the Europa League Final by losing to Dnipro 2-1 on aggregate. Having already adopted a strong Real Madrid influence in their own squad, the path connecting the two clubs was trodden in the other direction as Benítez departed Naples at the end of his contract for the Spanish giants. After the team had been developed and honed under Mazzarri, and then stagnated in Benítez's second season, it was reasonable to predict that De Laurentiis' next move would be for a high-calibre, household name to elevate Napoli into league title-winners. However, his next appointment would go completely against this grain.

The Luciano Spalletti Story:
Part One

IT IS hard not to be absorbed by Luciano Spalletti. His words swirl whilst referencing nature and history, building metaphors to summarise his unique perspectives on football. It might be the product of his upbringing in the Tuscan hills, in the town of Sovigliana, surrounded by farmland and rolling fields; where Spalletti still resides today and spent two years on sabbatical between 2019 and 2021.

Spalletti is a thinker. He ponders over minutiae and detail, but his demeanour and manner rarely reflect the forensic nature of his tactical mind. He smiles and laughs readily, shaking hands with journalists and opposition managers, and is now rarely seen not in a club branded tracksuit. There is an infectiousness about Luciano Spalletti that many do not find in other Italian managers of his generation. The steely, hard-nosed exteriors of Carlo Ancelotti, Massimiliano Allegri and Antonio Conte in many ways reflect their football. Pragmatic, difficult, and yet hyper-successful. Spalletti, for a long time, sat in a very different conversation to those three. His name would be grouped with those such as Gian Piero Gasperini and

Maurizio Sarri; ideologues whose legacy would depend upon context and tale beyond the binarism of silverware.

Spalletti's route into management was cultivated through a limited playing career in the lower divisions of Italian football. A rugged central midfielder, Spalletti was a late bloomer (making his professional debut at 23 with Castelfiorentino), but also a young retiree. He had stints with Entella, Viareggio, Spezia and Empoli in Serie C1 between 1985 and 1993, but called time on his playing career in 1993, aged 34. Spalletti's spell at his local side Empoli, which he had supported since childhood, was arguably what he was most renowned for prior to coaching. Tuscan journalist, writer, and Empoli fan Francesco Sani remembers Spalletti from his playing days at Empoli: 'Spalletti was a good second division midfielder, and arguably one of the best in Serie C1 at the time. He mixed elegance with strength and grit, and unsurprisingly had a great vision for the game. You don't see many players today of this profile and style.'

Spalletti was not the only member of that team to embark on a Serie A coaching journey. Vincenzo Montella, whose playing career impressed to a far greater extent than Spalletti's with spells at Roma and Sampdoria, can namecheck Fiorentina, Sampdoria, Milan and Sevilla on his own coaching résumé. 'Spalletti played in a beautiful Empoli team for those last two seasons of his career, with Montella in it, but it threw away two promotions so there aren't too many happy memories from that time!' remembers Francesco.

The transition into coaching was a natural and geographically convenient one for Spalletti as he assumed the role of Empoli manager in June 1993 upon ending his playing career with *Gli Azzurri* that same year and a spell with the academy. Remaining close to home, and within the club he loved, was the perfect role for Spalletti. So it proved, as Empoli and Spalletti flourished in each other's company. The club achieved back-to-back promotions in 1995/96, and then 1996/97 to lift them from Serie C1 into Serie A. In fact, Empoli were returning to the top flight for the first time since 1987/88, and it would be only their third ever season in Serie A. The grit and steel that had characterised Luciano Spalletti as a midfielder had carried over into his coaching style, creating a wily and reactive side that raced through the divisions in a manner few could have imagined. 'Spalletti's side was a mix of physicality, talent, and tactical intelligence,' recalls Francesco. 'It bore many similarities to Diego Simeone's Atletico Madrid, and played with two lethal strikers in Massimiliano Cappellini and Carmine Esposito.' Esposito especially was a star in Spalletti's side. In three seasons across Serie C1, Serie B and Serie A between 1996 and 1998, the forward scored 41 times in 92 appearances.

In his first senior management role, Luciano Spalletti had achieved something special with his beloved Empoli by bringing top division football to Stadio Carlo Castellani for the first time in a decade. Not that Spalletti was getting ahead of himself, however. If anything, the young coach felt overawed by the task at hand, and the speed at which he and his side had arrived at the highest level of Italian football. In an interview with *La Gazzetta dello Sport*, on the eve of Empoli's opening match of the season at home to Roma, Spalletti stated that he did not know if he was up to the challenge ahead. Empoli's performance against Fabio

Capello's brilliant Roma side, at a neutral Florentine venue, proved Spalletti had little to worry about. *Gli Azzurri* fell to a 3-1 defeat in valiant fashion, and created enough chances to threaten a side featuring the likes of Luigi Di Baglio, Cafu and Francesco Totti.

Empoli's reintroduction to Serie A could not have been tougher as they faced Roma, Napoli and Lazio in their first three matches before a Tuscan derby against Fiorentina followed in the fourth matchweek. They emerged from that run with six points, with a 1-0 home win over Lazio marking Spalletti's first-ever Serie A victory, followed up immediately with a 2-1 win in the Derby dell'Arno. The roller-coaster return rolled on, and inconsistency marked the first half of Empoli's season. A 1-1 draw with Inter as winter drew on demonstrated Empoli's growing confidence to mix it with the established giants of Serie A, and a 4-3 thriller at Stadio Olimpico nearly avenged that opening-day defeat to Roma.

Without a doubt, however, the result of Empoli's season was a 5-0 win over Napoli. Admittedly, this was a poor Napoli side that would end the season bottom of the table. However, playing with a spikiness and bite, Empoli ran amok to register their largest score of the campaign. Such margins of victory would prove crucial by the season's end. At this time Serie A comprised of 18 rather than today's customary 20 clubs, and the bottom four (rather than bottom three) would all be relegated. With the top nine securing European football in some capacity across Champions League, UEFA Cup, Cup Winners' Cup and Intertoto Cup, the line between relegation and historic achievement could not have been closer. Seven points from their final four matches secured Empoli safety in 13th place on 37 points, as Brescia (35), Atalanta (32), Lecce (26) and Napoli (14) all fell down into Serie B. Such was the unusual make-up of the division that season, only five teams finished campaign with neither relegation nor European football, in a halfway zone between extremes. Two points above the drop, and nine points adrift of Sampdoria in ninth, Empoli had achieved salvation on their return. Their 50 goals was bettered only by the top nine (even Milan in tenth scored fewer), and was the major contributor to their survival. Only four teams, including three of the relegated four, conceded more than their 58 goals. If Empoli were to go again and build upon such an achievement the following season, defensive solidity would have to be addressed.

This task would not be undertaken by coach Luciano Spalletti. Sampdoria had been impressed by the then 39-year-old. Having fired two managers since the start of the 1997/98 season (1978 FIFA World Cup-winning coach César Luis Menotti, and then Vujadin Boškov), the club turned to Spalletti to become their new head coach. 'After two promotions and one salvation, the cycle had come to an end,' says Francesco. 'It is important to underline that Spalletti saved Empoli in Serie A, at a time where *calcio* ruled world football.' A young manager, in his first senior position, had secured the Serie A safety of a club with only two prior seasons in the top division, in the world's toughest league at the time.

The legacy of Spalletti at Empoli is almost untouchable, explains Francesco. When asked where Spalletti ranks in the history of Empoli managers, he replies, 'Number one of course! Maurizio Sarri comes second for his promotion to Serie A in 2013/14, and special mentions to Gaetano Salvemini and Silvio Baldini. But Spalletti is the best.'

The connection between Luciano Spalletti and Empoli is deep-rooted, and continued beyond his coaching spell. 'After the Sampdoria job, Spalletti went back to his hometown of Sovigliana and coached the local team in his spare time. The club's headquarters are in a bar called "The House of People", and Spalletti would frequently go there and talk about football with other customers. He is simply known as "Luciano" there!'

Having experienced a modest playing career, and moving into management at the local club he supported, Luciano Spalletti would now be tested at one of the cornerstones of Italian football. A four-time Coppa Italia winner, UEFA Cup Winners' Cup victors in 1989/90, and Serie A champions as recently as 1990/91, Sampdoria were a different beast altogether. Their ninth-place finish in 1997/98 was their lowest since 1985/86 (11th), and with a squad far weaker than that spearheaded by Gianluca Vialli and Roberto Mancini a few years before, Spalletti was tasked with maintaining the standard expected.

Spalletti was brought back down to earth with a bump. Sampdoria won only three of their first 13 league matches of the 1998/99 season, and following a bruising 5-2 loss away to Lazio, Spalletti was fired and replaced with former player David Platt. The change in manager did nothing to arrest the slide and Sampdoria picked up a measly three points from their next possible 18, without winning a match. In a turn of events only Italian football can conjure, *La Samp* relieved Platt of his duties following this dreadful run, and reappointed Spalletti in a desperate bid to save their season. The 1981/82 season was the last time they had been relegated, and whilst Spalletti improved on his previous spell with six wins and three draws across the final 15 weeks of the season, it wasn't enough. Only nine points separated Sampdoria in 16th from Inter in eighth in another tightly contested relegation battle. The nature of Sampdoria's condemnation to the second tier made it all the more painful. With two fixtures remaining, Sampdoria required better results than one of either Salernitana or Perugia, with one or both likely to be relegated should Sampdoria survive. All three sides took four points from their last two matches, but Sampdoria were within seconds of having six were it not for a 95th-minute penalty by Bologna's Klas Ingesson to level the scores at 2-2. Had they held on and won that penultimate match at Stadio Renato Dall'Ara, they would have switched places with Perugia and survived on goal difference.

Such hypotheticals could not stave off the reality that Sampdoria had fallen from a great height, Serie A champions just eight years before, to playing in Serie B for the turn of the millennium. For the second time in six months, Luciano Spalletti was fired by Sampdoria. However, unlike his previous employers, Spalletti would remain in Serie A for the next campaign. Still only 40 years old, Spalletti was one of Italy's brightest young coaches and the memories of his Empoli successes were fresh in the mind. Sampdoria's relegation could not be placed on his shoulders, and the problems resulting in their relegation extended far beyond a young manager in just his second senior posting.

Venezia had been promoted to Serie A for the 1998/99 campaign, pulling themselves clear of relegation danger with an improved second half of the season following a dire beginning. Despite the great escape, and having won promotion back to the top division for the first time in over three decades, manager Walter Novellino was fired by owner Maurizio Zamparini, and replaced by Spalletti for the following season.

The ingredients were there for Venezia to develop into a stable Serie A side. Sporting director Beppe Marotta, who would go on to become one of Italy's most influential boardroom figures with spells at Sampdoria, Juventus and Inter, had bolstered the squad for the previous year with young Inter loanee Álvaro Recoba and goalkeeper Massimo Taibi from Milan. Both had left by the time Spalletti could take charge of his first match, but Marotta's eye for talent plus Zamparini's desire to hire young, progressive managers, and the capacity to develop Venice as a 'football city', was a promising mix. Recruitment ahead of Spalletti's first season, however, paled in comparison to the one that came before, as neither Taibi nor Recoba were adequately replaced. Venezia lost seven of their opening ten Serie A matches, with a shock 1-0 win over Inter marking their only victory between late August and December 1999. The day after a 1-0 loss at home to Bologna, Zamparini subjected Spalletti to his third sacking in almost 12 months. The situation was alarmingly similar to his spell at Sampdoria, and Zamparini's reputation for hiring and firing in quick succession meant there was little hope for Spalletti to rectify the dire predicament facing the club.

The late Zamparini garnered an infamous reputation in Italian football. A colourful character who was never afraid to speak his mind to the press, Zamparini was renowned for his ability to act on impulse and undermine his managers. As owner of Palermo in 2012 for example, he fired and then re-hired Gian Piero Gasperini in the space of 19 days. Gasperini had only started in the role four months prior, and would be sacked again in March 2013.

Back in 1999/2000, Zamparini was making identical decisions. With Spalletti sacked, Zamparini turned to Giuseppe Materazzi, who lasted all of 27 days in the job before Spalletti was re-hired. At Sampdoria, Spalletti's second spell had yielded improved results if not enough to secure safety. In Venice too, three wins in six matches followed his reappointment going into the new year. It was not long before the looming finger of Zamparini acted again, however. Two heavy losses (5-2 to Udinese and 5-0 at Roma) in three weeks were enough to see Spalletti relieved once more. Zamparini in an interview many years later acknowledged Spalletti's prowess as a coach, but had acted off a sense that he was 'bad luck'. In an interview with Radio Kiss Kiss Napoli in 2019 (cited by *Forza Italian Football*), Zamparini declared that: 'He [Spalletti] always wore black. I called him an undertaker, and I told hm he was bad luck. Against Torino we were 2-0 up in the 90th minute, then we drew 2-2. I sacked him because I thought it was bad luck.' Like Sampdoria before them, Venezia were duly relegated.

The positivity and promise Spalletti had ridden off the back of his time at Empoli was creeping further and further away into the rearview mirror. At Sampdoria and Venezia, Spalletti had been hired to save sides from relegation, and ultimately failed both times across four combined stints. Spalletti was caught in a cycle. Few who witnessed the events in Genoa and Venice could have seriously levelled blame at such a young manager at the expense of acknowledging the long-standing flaws at each club. The cycle was soon to continue too, as Spalletti was hired by Udinese in the spring of 2001 to try and arrest relegation once more. Out of the frying pan, into the fire. Like Zamparini before, the Pozzo family that owned Udinese were ruthless in their hiring-and-firing policy. Spalletti was to become the club's fourth head coach in as many years. *Le Zebrette* had experienced the recent highs of European football, playing in the UEFA Cup for the first time in 1997/98 under manager Alberto Zaccheroni, and featuring German international Oliver Bierhoff. 'Bierhoff and Márcio Amoroso were world class players under Zaccheroni,' remembers Mattia Montanaro, a lifelong Udinese fan. A third-place finish that season resulted in Zaccheroni and Bierhoff both departing for Milan, and neither his successor Francesco Guidolin nor the next incumbent Luigi De Canio could stabilise the side in the face of such losses. With just two months of the Serie A season remaining, and Udinese facing the real threat of relegation, Spalletti was hired to replace De Canio.

If Spalletti's recent experiences had felt like a case of rinsing and repeating, the 2000/01 season was about to break the cycle. Udinese lost three of his first five in charge, including three successive matches against Milan, Roma and Fiorentina. With that treacherous run complete, Udinese lost only two of their final six matches; drawing three and winning once. Survival was achieved on the penultimate weekend of the season, away at Atalanta. A 31st-minute winner from Roberto Muzzi guaranteed *Le Zebrette*'s safety, and Spalletti's curse had been broken. Those delusions and expectations of European football, stemming back even to the 1980s when Zico wore the black and white of Udine, hampered any great sense of salvation, however.

'The team was still an average one under Spalletti,' says Mattia. 'The fans were still dreaming of those wonderful European nights of years before, but they had lost hope as neither the coach nor the teams of recent years had managed to improve. There was no sense of love for Spalletti, even if he succeeded in avoiding relegation.'

Spalletti had achieved his most notable success in three years since leaving Empoli, yet it was still not enough to keep him in a job. The Pozzos relieved Spalletti of his duties, and replaced him with Roy Hodgson. Endemic of the underlying issues at Udinese, even the experience of Hodgson failed to produce an uplift. 'After a good start, the season ended even worse than the previous one,' remembers Mattia. Hodgson was fired in December, and his successor Gian Piero Ventura did not last beyond the end of the season. It was time to bring back Luciano Spalletti.

Prior to accepting the position, Spalletti had taken a year away from the limelight. The 2001/02 season saw him coach Serie B side Ancona, and manage *I Dorici* to a respectable eighth-place finish. A stunning beachside city on the eastern coast of Italy, kissed by warm Adriatic waters, Ancona allowed Spalletti the respite needed after a tumultuous and taxing period of his career.

The lure of Serie A was too much to resist, however. Spalletti had unfinished business in righting the wrongs of the previous few years, and to build upon his first stint in Udine. The tangibly underwhelming feeling among fans transpired into an equally low-key start to Spalletti's second spell. The first ten matches yielded a mere nine points, with 1-0 victories over Atalanta and Reggina being *Le Zebrette's* only wins alongside defeats to Piacenza, Roma, Juventus and Milan. A fifth loss in 11 appeared to be looming at San Siro when Christian Vieri put Inter ahead after three minutes. What followed, however, would come to shape Udinese and Luciano Spalletti forever. Martin Jørgensen and Roberto Muzzi both scored to turn the match, and gift a precious win. From there, Udinese would lose only two of their next ten Serie A fixtures, winning four in that time (a 2-0 win away at Como was awarded after fan rioting led to the match's abandonment). The results and consistency had turned in their favour, and Spalletti was beginning to impose his blueprint on a team for an extended period for the first time since leaving Tuscany. He had settled on a three-man defence, with aggressive wing-backs and inverted wingers, and high technical quality in central midfield. What was interesting, however, was that the Udinese squad did not have the profiles of player to fill such positions. Or so one thought.

A perfect example of how Spalletti sought to repurpose his squad was the case of David Pizarro, a Chilean international who had been loaned back to Chile for the previous season. Diminutive in stature, Pizarro excelled in ball-carrying, and would often be used in more advanced areas as a result. Spalletti had other ideas, and sought to utilise Pizarro's excellent ball control and reading of space by playing him as a deep-lying midfielder; a *regista*. 'Pizarro had shown glimpses of talent but had hardly flourished. Turning him into a *regista* felt counter-intuitive at first as Pizarro was a much better carrier than passer,' explains Mattia. Across the season, only goalkeeper Morgan De Sanctis (3,060) played more Serie A minutes for Udinese than Pizarro, and this unique deployment of skill set would reappear many years later in several different Spalletti sides. Pizarro would gather the ball deep from the defence, almost between centre-backs, and slow the tempo down to invite high pressure from the opponents. In doing so, and drawing them forward, space would open between the lines for Pizarro to carry or pass into. It was a development that Mattia remembers as being 'ahead of its time'.

Another shift saw new signing Marek Jankulovski rotated between wing-back and left wing according on the opposition and the attacking licence that could be afforded to the Czech. Young forward Vincenzo Iaquinta had spent much of his time on the left of the attack, but Spalletti redesigned his game to play centrally. Iaquinta now offered pace and direct running into the penalty area, and could stretch defences by moving into wide channels. Without being prolific, seven goals was a worthy return for a developing forward in his first campaign in a new role.

This trio were the shining lights in an excellent season. Jankulovski provided directness, either from the left as a wing-back, or cutting in from the right flank to cross or rocket shots goalwards. A 2-0 win at home to Perugia on the penultimate matchweek showcased such a skill set. The Czech gathered the ball between the Perugia midfield and defensive lines, turned quickly to move towards the opposition goal, and rifled an unstoppable effort into the bottom corner without it touching the floor. That result came late in a superb run of form towards the tail-end of the season. Udinese won five of their last six matches, pipping Chievo Verona to sixth place by a single point, thus qualifying for the UEFA Cup first round. Chievo's dramatic 4-3 defeat to Juventus on the final day allowed Udinese to usurp them with a 2-1 victory over Lazio. Sure enough, it was a penalty from Pizarro and a Jankulovski piledriver that secured the three points and booked Udinese's spot in Europe for the first time since 1998/99. This was the calibre of achievement Spalletti had been yearning for; no longer a relegation-battling firefighter, but pushing sides towards the upper mid-table and above. The act was repeated the following season when a seventh-place finish guaranteed back-to-back UEFA Cup qualifications for Udinese, despite receiving limited investment from the Pozzos during the summer. Their European run that campaign was short-lived, beating SV Austria Salzburg (now known as RB Salzburg) 1-0 away from home before falling to a 2-1 defeat in Austria to be knocked out in the first round.

It had become apparent that Spalletti's Udinese were a vicious thorn in the side of the biggest clubs. Neither Milan nor Inter beat *Le Zebrette* across four matches that season, as Udinese won twice at San Siro. At a time when Italian football was deep into an era of highly structured style, and teams being built off the back of tight reactive defences, Udinese offered something different. They played with a swagger and arrogance that belied their stature, and a bravery in the opposition's half that could knock stronger sides off kilter. Through the lens of today's football, where structures of positional play rule over the individual exploits of the individual, it looks rugged and often reckless. Midfielders look up and shoot from range with regularity rather than seeking to manufacture the perfect opening, and possession sequences are kept short before switching play into space with booming cross-field passes. As mentioned, however, it was exactly this sort of direct verve exhibited by Udinese that stunned the opposition. Yet the glass ceiling that had only been raised just a season before was about to be smashed through once again.

* * *

Sunday, 29 May 2005. The battle for fourth place and Champions League qualification had reached the final match of the season. Udinese sat in fourth, having to equal or better fifth-placed Sampdoria's result to qualify for the first time. The problem was that they faced the might of Milan, whilst *La Samp* had the much easier task of playing relegation-battling Bologna. The tension was palpable, and remembered well by Mattia Montanaro: 'If we had beaten Cagliari the previous week, fourth was ours. Sadly we threw the chance away, drew 1-1 and I remember feeling so sad. It came down to the last match of the season on a hot day at Stadio Friuli. I am a nine-year-old kid there with his dad to support in the Curva Nord. Everyone was so tense, listening to the radio for news from the Sampdoria match. It was the longest 90 minutes of my life.'

David Di Michele had been Udinese's top scorer that season with an impressive 15 Serie A strikes. It was the Italian centre-forward that gave *La Zebrette* the lead against Milan, spinning away from two challengers to drive forward and lash a low finish past goalkeeper Dida. Still no news came from Bologna, as the match crept into its final throes. Hearts were set racing when Milan equalised in the 88th minute, meaning a late Sampdoria goal would see them leap into fourth. With ears glued to radios, the referee blows for full-time in Udine. 'Everyone is desperate to know the result and whether Sampdoria managed to nick a late goal. Then came the announcement … 0-0! We are fourth! Everyone runs on the pitch, hugging each other. The city was full of *bianconero* (black and white) dresses partying and chanting, klaxons and car horns blaring. Even now, that moment gives me shivers.'

Udinese and Luciano Spalletti had qualified for the Champions League. They had finished on 62 points, 12 better than the previous Serie A campaign, and restored the memories of decades before. The Pozzo family's investments had been validated, as they had brought in forwards Antonio Di Natale and Di Michele (back from a loan spell at Reggina) to bolster their attack. Between them and Iaquinta, the trio scored 35 and assisted 14 as Udinese metamorphosised into Spalletti's perfect vision.

The next step, taking Udinese into their first ever Champions League campaign, was not to be Spalletti's to undertake. His work in Udine had attracted interest from Roma, by far the largest club of Spalletti's career at that point. Their proposal, plus mitigating factors surrounding his current employers, made the decision for Spalletti. Mattia tells me: 'He [Spalletti] knew that the Pozzo family would sell some key players as they always do. The method of selling their best players for a lot of money, and bringing cheap youngsters in works for the club's bank account, but not for a coach embarking on his first Champions League season.' It is a dilemma that presents itself to young, ambitious coaches across the world. Do they continue to enjoy the comforts of their current project, where they are loved and respected for what they have achieved with limited resources? Or leave and test themselves at an institution the size of Roma, and make the next step? Spalletti chose the latter, telling *Gazzetta dello Sport* (via *World Soccer*) just days after the 2004/05 season ended: 'I consider my cycle at Udinese to have concluded. I don't feel I am able to guarantee fourth place every year for the club. The thought it won't be me on the bench when Udinese play in the Champions League saddens me, I can't deny that.' Despite the success he had achieved, Spalletti's decision to leave and damp Udinese's glorious moment left a sour taste. 'Every ti Spalletti has come back to play in Udine, he receive welcome and is booed. His decision to leave turned from a legend into a traitor.'

* * *

Rome. The Eternal City. An iconic destinatio rich tapestry into which are woven history, m food, arts and football. Roma are seen from th as being Rome's club, despite cohabiting with and both sitting within the famed 'Seven Siste football' group. The 2004/05 season had been one for *I Giallorossi* (the yellow and reds), cy four managers and ending the league sea place. A Coppa Italia final appearance di over a dreadful season both on and off t lost Scudetto-winning coach Fabio Capello before it had begun, and a darkening financial situation: not the calmest of environments for Luciano Spalletti to walk into. It could have been stormier too, when the club were punished with a transfer ban for agreeing a deal with AJ Auxerre defender Philippe Mexes that saw him move to Rome in 2004, despite still being under contract with his club. The club had acted swiftly by signing multiple players before the transfer ban arrived, meaning the effects were limited.

Spalletti's introduction to Stadio Olimpico could not have been better scripted by a Hollywood director. He had won his first Serie A match away at Reggina, and his home debut followed with former side Udinese his opponent. Naturally, *Le Zebrette* avenged their fans' broken hearts by beating Spalletti in front of his new employers, a defeat that began a patchy run for the Tuscan as he settled into Roman life. Only two victories came in his first eight Serie A matches at the helm.

An away trip to Inter's San Siro saw the tide turn as Spalletti continued his impressive record at Italy's most iconic stadium. Roma emerged 3-2 victors, but it was the manner of the win that impressed most. Spalletti had not had his perfect line-up yet, and was yet to find a perfect role for captain Francesco Totti. Vincenzo Montella remained the starting centre-forward, so Totti started as the link between Montella and the midfield. With Daniele De Rossi posting deepest in central midfield when Roma had possession, Totti had the licence to either drop in deep to receive the ball and pick a pass in space, or join the forward line in shape (with Totti included as one of the midfield 'four') that would come to define Spalletti's tenure, albeit with one major adjustment. When Inter had the ball, De Rossi's midfield partner Simone Perrotta would snap forward from his deep position to press in line with Montella, Totti and the winger nearest to the ball. Inter could not handle the ferocity, and winning the ball in their half allowed Roma to get the ball to Totti as quickly as possible.

In the match's 30th minute, Roma won possession inside their half and fed Totti on the halfway line. The captain rode two challenges and strode on as Inter retreated, gliding towards the centre of Inter's half. With Julio Cesar off his goal line, Totti clipped the most nonchalant of finishes over the Brazilian's desperate backwards fall. It was the type of goal only Totti could score. German manager Jürgen Klopp once stated that an effective counter-press (pressing aggressively to win the ball immediately after losing it, rather than settling back into an out-of-possession shape), was as effective at creating chances as fielding a creative player behind the striker. Spalletti and Roma had both in their arsenal.

As the season wore on and *I Giallorossi* climbed the table, Spalletti made his bravest call. Montella's strike against Inter was his only goal of the Serie A season. Rather than replace the increasingly erratic centre-forward with another striker, Spalletti moved Totti forward and instead introduced another central midfielder. The 4-1-4-1 shape remained, but the way it would be played changed.

Totti was far from the archetypal centre-forward. Arguably Serie A's most talented player during his extensive career, Totti combined grace and jaw-dropping technicalability with brutal ball-striking, and an awareness of space that few could match. Spalletti's vision was to start Totti as the furthest player forward, and drop him deep to allow the midfield to rush beyond him and attack the penalty box with vertical runs. Totti had the ability to thread passes through the eye of a needle, or take on the opportunity himself. Either way, his movement was a nightmare for opponents to deal with. Centre-backs were accustomed to having the opposition striker back into them and contend physically, not pull towards the midfield. Equally, the midfield could not follow Totti as he moved across the pitch, as that created space for the likes of De Rossi and Perrotta in central areas. Spalletti's use of Totti in this way is identified as one of the first uses of the 'false nine'. By the season's end, Totti had 15 goals and nine assists to his name from 24 Serie A appearances.

Spalletti was christened a genius as Roma went 13 matches unbeaten between December and March; a run that included an 11-match winning run that equalled the league record. The 2005/06 season was the campaign rocked by the *Calciopoli* scandal, and saw league leaders Juventus along with second-place Milan punished (relegation for the former, a 30-point deduction for the latter). This propelled Roma into second place with their tally of 69 points, and despite losing the then-two-legged Coppa Italia Final to Inter, presented a positive first season in the capital for Luciano Spalletti.

A star of Spalletti's previous side would be joining up with him in Rome for the next season. David Pizarro's transformation into a tempo-setting central midfielder was pivotal to his successes at Udinese, so Roma sought to reunite the pair at Stadio Olimpico with Pizarro as the club's marquee signing that summer. Doing so allowed Totti to push further forward into the nominal 'false nine' position while Simone Perrotta filled the creative space behind, and Pizarro could sit alongside De Rossi in a balanced central pivot. The result was spectacular, as Spalletti's blueprint hit new heights. *I Giallorossi* lost just four of their first 24 Serie A matches, going on a similar run of wins to that record-equalling stretch in 2005/06. The defence also improved, conceding eight fewer goals than in the previous campaign at less than a goal per match across the season. Were it not for an all-conquering Inter under Roberto Mancini hitting 97 points and losing just one league match, Roma might have found themselves in a serious title race. Their form dropped off significantly in the late-season run-in, something that has dogged Luciano Spalletti throughout his career. Defeats to Atalanta, Torino and Cagliari in the last six fixtures were a blemish on a fantastic season that hit its peak on 9 May 2007.

In their second Coppa Italia final against Inter in as many years, having lost the previous iteration, Roma demolished one of the era's most dominant teams. In the first leg at Stadio Olimpico, a 6-2 mauling all but guaranteed a first major trophy of Spalletti's career. Only once before has a side scored six in a Coppa Italia Final (1994, Sampdoria 6-1 Ancona), let alone against Scudetto-winning Inter. Totti opened the scoring inside a minute, setting the tone for a brutal attacking tornado to sweep across their home turf. De Rossi added a second just four minutes later by flicking home Philippe Mexes' fierce volley, before Perrotta rounded off a sweeping counter-attack on 15 minutes. It was Roma in full poetic motion in the scorching sun of the capital. Having remained motionless for the first two, Spalletti leapt into the air in delirium at Perrotta's goal. De Rossi and Pizarro marked Inter's midfield pair man-to-man, beating them to the ball and firing vertical passes through the lines to find Totti. With Totti dropping into that between-line space, Roma's midfield became a diamond shape with Totti at the tip, and wide players Taddei and Mancini running beyond. Perrotta too would run beyond Totti, doing so to poke home left-back Christian Chivu's cross. The motion and movement on show could not be contained by Inter.

A 2-1 defeat at Stadio Giuseppe Meazza was insufficient to overturn the result, and Roma were crowned Coppa Italia champions for the first time in 26 years. Spalletti too had his first piece of major silverware, but it was the manner and style of his team that won admiration as much as the significance of winning the final. Totti's reputation was already sky-high in Rome, but across Europe he was now as revered as at any point in his career. The club captain scored 26 and assisted nine in Serie A, aided by five converted penalties but also hindered by a further missed five. He finished tenth in the 2007 Ballon d'Or vote, too. Online publication *The Gentleman Ultra* quoted Spalletti's own interview in 2012 with *Gazzetta Dello Sport* on his innovation in remodelling Totti's role: 'Moving Francesco closer to the box was like putting the fox near to the henhouse: he always finds the space to create panic amongst the opposition. Totti can score and provide assists, with every kick he can find small spaces.'

The running battles between Mancini's Inter and Spalletti's Roma were far from done. *I Giallorossi* picked up where they left off the very next season, losing just one Serie A match in the first 21 matchweeks. That one defeat? A 4-1 humbling at Stadio Olimpico to *I Nerazzurri*. Away from Serie A, Spalletti's Roma proved to be a nuisance in Champions League competition. They had begun to build an impressive body of European work a year previous, finishing second in their group and eliminating Lyon in the round of 16. In the quarter-finals, they even beat Manchester United 2-1 at Stadio Olimpico to ignite dreams of a semi-final run. However, their impressive ascent was doused in a deluge of water at Old Trafford as Sir Alex Ferguson's side put seven past them in Manchester. The significance of this to the following season was that the two sides were drawn in the same group to re-live their remarkable two-legged tie of a year before. The Red Devils won the first at Old Trafford 1-0, and the second was a 1-1 draw, a far cry from the 11 goals shared in 2006/07.

Roma once again came second in their group to progress. From there, Roma were drawn against Real Madrid. A European fixture against *Los Blancos* needs little constructed narrative; their aura carries more than enough weight for that to be required. On this occasion though, recent history elevated the interest. Francesco Totti had been heavily rumoured to be on the cusp of a move to the Spanish capital in both 2004 and 2006. His loyalty and the adoration of Rome perhaps made Totti the only Galactico that was truly out of reach for Real Madrid.

Whilst this was not a vintage Real Madrid side, and one that would have been unlikely to threaten in the latter stages, Roma beat them over two legs. Both matches were won with a 2-1 scoreline, and the second at Santiago

Bernabéu was aided by the home side's reduction to ten men. Nevertheless, it sealed Roma's place in the quarter-finals for the second successive season at the expense of the competition's most successful club. To this day, it arguably remains Spalletti's most important result in Europe, and sealed the Totti–Real situation with a kiss. However, their progress was to be stunted yet again by Manchester United in the pair's fifth and sixth meetings in two seasons. Roma were spared the bashing the Red Devils had administered a year before, but a 3-0 aggregate defeat again closed the door on semi-final dreams.

Their exit allowed Roma to concentrate on the unenviable task of catching Inter in the race for the Scudetto. Once again, they fell short despite losing just one of their last ten matches in the league. Mancini's Inter lost twice in this time, but were already too far ahead having been unbeaten until the 26th matchweek. Roma finished an agonising three points behind in second, and a disappointing run of results at the turn of 2008 had ultimately cost them against a winning machine. Inter's dominance would extend for another two years as Roberto Mancini was replaced by José Mourinho, who added European glory to the plethora of Serie A titles accumulated in the recent past. Their incessant winning would prove too much for Spalletti, but we'll come to that later.

Spalletti and Mancini would have one final showdown before the latter departed Inter. For the third season in a row, the pair would face off in the Coppa Italia Final, having won one apiece. The competition had reverted to a one-match final in place of the two-legged affairs, and

Spalletti would have the final laugh. His trusty lieutenant David Pizarro was at the heart of things, whipping a short and low corner for Philippe Mexes to hammer home first time. The second goal was beautifully constructed by Simone Perrotta, Ludovic Giuly and Mirko Vučinić and the latter converted into an unguarded net. The absence of the injured Francesco Totti was not felt as Roma won back-to-back Coppa Italia titles. Roma and Spalletti had elevated themselves into the next contender position. Their beautiful Totti-inspired football was now winning trophies and had pushed a great side to the very end. With Mancini now gone, Roma could aim for the Scudetto. Little did they know of the Mourinho-shaped tornado that was heading their way.

The Portuguese turned Inter from a domestic giant into a European one by winning the title in 2008/09, and then the treble in 2009/10. Somehow, Mourinho had gone beyond Mancini's achievements and that era of Inter brilliance is almost solely remembered for Mourinho's role and not his predecessor's. Another obstacle to Roma's ambitions was the declining fitness of Totti. Having suffered separate knee and cruciate ligament injuries in 2007/08, Spalletti's captain and star player would incur a further five different injuries the next year. Roma had become so reliant on Totti's brilliance that they could not function without him, and Spalletti had forgotten what it was like to field a conventional striker. They lost six of their opening nine matches, and Spalletti was starting to lose the dressing room. Totti later stated that Spalletti 'couldn't make himself understood anymore'. Players began to feel alienated, and whilst technical director Rosella Sensi was supplying the players Spalletti wanted, few could be deemed successful in Rome.

A brilliant deep dive on Spalletti's Roma by Roma fan site *Chiesa Di Totti* states that Spalletti's methods were being questioned. Players were sent home with coaching manuals to revise, and training involved 11 vs 11 matches to essentially cultivate two separate and diasporic teams. It wasn't working any more, and a sixth-place finish in 2008/09 marked the end of Roma's success in the late 2000s. The writing was on the wall, and it was a surprise to many that Spalletti stayed on until the start of the 2009/10 season. It drew out a painful end of what had been a largely successful spell for both coach and club. Two defeats to Genoa and Juventus to begin the next season broke the situation wide open as Spalletti resigned, and it would be nearly seven years before he coached in Italy again. Totti had the last word, writing in his autobiography that Spalletti was one of the few coaches who pushed him to work harder rather than allowing him to be himself and let his performances speak for themselves. 'That annoyed me a little', wrote Totti. He also lavished the incoming Claudio Ranieri with praise, which seemingly only worsened the outside perspective of Spalletti's downfall at Roma. A narrative between Totti and Spalletti was being built, and would lie dormant for most of the next decade before exploding.

The Luciano Spalletti Story:
Part Two

LUCIANO SPALLETTI has never been a conformist. His track record speaks of a coach that follow his heart over his head, of what is right over what is easy. Quick tone changes and pivots turn Spalletti away from the conventional and throw him into a new, unforeseen challenge. Having spent 11 years at difficult Italian sides before reaching Roma, perhaps the trickiest and most political of all, Spalletti was choosing his own destiny.

Very few would have anticipated that Spalletti would not coach again in Italy until 2016. Aside from Roberto Mancini, Carlo Ancelotti and Fabio Capello, the top European sides were veering away from Italian coaches at the time. Even within Italy Ancelotti had left Milan at the end of the 2008/09 season for Chelsea, and was succeeded by a Brazilian, Leonardo. At Inter, José Mourinho was the new man on the touchline following Mancini's departure. Spalletti was different to those names, firstly by virtue of trophies and experience, but also in his perception of the game. Mancini, Ancelotti and Capello were serial winners, and adjusted their methods according to the players at hand and getting them to perform to a winning standard. Spalletti was an ideologue. His aim was to bend a club or team to his will in order to play his football. At Udinese and his first three seasons in Rome, this had been a successful approach: in 2006 and 2007 he had been recognised as Serie A Coach of the Year. However, the latter years at Roma had worn Spalletti down. The weight of expectation, the in-fighting, and having to carry the burden for a physically declining Francesco Totti; it ground Spalletti down and his footballing philosophy suffered as a result. He needed a fresh start.

The 2000s saw an unprecedented wave of money start flowing into Russian football. Gazprom, a state-owned energy company that would become a key sponsor of the UEFA Champions League from 2012 to 2022, began investing heavily alongside Russian oligarchs and businesses into the Russian game. Gazprom bought a 70% stake in Zenit St Petersburg, and by 2010 their investment had returned one Russian Premier League title, a Super Cup, and the 2007/08 UEFA Cup and UEFA Super Cup. Coached by Dutch manager Dick Advocaat, Zenit had become a domestic force and European regular with a mostly Russian squad (record signing Portuguese midfielder Danny aside) and led by talismanic forwards Andrey Arshavin and Pavel Pogrebnyak. However, the tide turned quickly on Advocaat as a third-place finish and a Champions League exit in 2009 saw him relieved of his duties after three years in charge. Zenit were seventh at the time of Advocaat's dismissal, and he was sacked despite having already agreed in principle to leave at the end of the season to coach the Belgian national side. Arshavin and Pogrebnyak left for Arsenal and VfB Stuttgart respectively, and interim coach Anatoli Davydov steered the Zenit ship to third position. Davydov was kept at the club, having been head coach of the reserves prior to his promotion to caretaker manager.

Just three months after leaving Roma, Luciano Spalletti was named as the new head coach of Zenit St Petersburg on a three-year contract. On the surface it appeared to be a drastic gear change from the trials and tribulations of coaching in Rome, but the two projects bore similarities: enormous clubs sitting just outside of where they wanted to be, with recent cup success but lacking the sustained period of consistency at the top of their respective leagues. The difference with Zenit was that Spalletti now had serious financial backing, when at Roma he had grown frustrated by a lack of transfer activity.

Spalletti took his time to warm up in Russia. In eight winter friendlies heading into the 2010 season, Zenit lost four and won three. Even by the sixth week of the Russian Premier League season, the 2007/08 UEFA Cup champions were yet to hit their stride as they drew three of their opening six, scoring just four times. A 2-0 away win at CSKA Moscow proved to be the turning point as it set Zenit on a run of nine successive victories either side of the mid-season break. After moving to the top of the table in matchweek nine, Zenit stayed there for the rest of the season, and would drop just 16 points across the remaining 22 matches of the league season. The only disappointment was a 2-1 aggregate defeat to French side Auxerre in the Champions League play-off round, sending Zenit into the Europa League (formerly UEFA Cup) for the season. Gazprom flexed their financial muscle to supply Spalletti with Portuguese international centre-back Bruno Alves, Russian attacker Aleksandr Bukharov and Serbian Aleksandar Luković for a combined €40 million. They will have been pleased with their investment, both in the squad and in their new coach, as Zenit won their first league title since 2007 and secured the Russian Cup to complete a domestic double. The team had already begun to take on Spalletti's image, too. They played in a 4-3-3 with the midfield split between an advanced creator and a base of two energetic protectors. Zenit would press high, with one of the midfield joining the front line to cover all passing angles when an opponent played out from the back.

Spalletti's influence also began to tell in the transfer market as Zenit signed Italian centre-back Domenico Criscito. The transfer of Criscito was seen as an impressive coup, stealing a capped 25-year-old defender away from Serie A. That Criscito had come through the ranks at Genoa, then spent time at Juventus before returning to Genoa and developing under Gian Piero Gasperini, only furthered the sense that Spalletti was recruiting a centre-back to elevate his side's ball-playing capacity.

Zenit carried over their previous season's imperious form, losing just twice in their first ten Premier League matches (one of which was an awarded 3-0 win to CSKA Moscow, due to Zenit not fielding a player born after 1990 in their line-up). This would turn out to be their worst patch of domestic form in an incredible season during which they would lose only once more in the league. The 2011 season was used as a transition for the Russian Premier League as it moved away from its old format of playing from spring to autumn with a mid-season summer break. It would now start in autumn, finish in spring and feature a midwinter break to avoid playing in the year's harshest conditions. The idea behind this was to align Russia's domestic game with the rest of Europe, as participation in UEFA competitions would effectively eradicate any break between seasons for the Russian sides and campaigns would merge together.

In order for this new model to be implemented, the 2011 season carried on into 2012 with the division split into two sets of eight according to their placings at the end of the regular season with each group playing each other twice more. At the end of this enormous 44-match season, Zenit finished seven points clear at the top to win their second successive Premier League title. Whilst they failed to defend their Russian Cup title, a Russian Super Cup was added to the club's silverware collection and a commendable run in the Champions League offered promise of Zenit becoming a regular contributor to Europe's premier competition. Drawn in an undaunting group with APOEL of Cyprus, Porto and Shakhtar Donetsk, Zenit progressed in second place behind the Cypriots on goal difference. A 4-3 aggregate defeat to Benfica in the next round showed real promise after winning the first-leg 3-2 in St Petersburg, but equally galling for not sealing qualification across both matches.

The financial might behind Spalletti showed its face ahead of the 2012 season. With the calendar now amended to improve Russian performances in Europe, Zenit set about luring some of the continent's brightest talents to Russia. The most notable arrival was that of Hulk, a powerful Brazilian winger who had scored four goals in the Champions League for Porto a season before and had been heavily linked with a move to Chelsea. Reports of the fee paid range from €40-€60 million, and an annual salary of €8 million set eyes watering in a Russian record transfer that would stand for seven years. This was not the first time Hulk had taken an unexpected turn in his career, having played in Japan for three years before joining Porto in 2008. The interest in Hulk was huge. He was a devastating attacker with one of the most powerful ball-striking abilities seen in the game, and a regular at international level with Brazil.

Zenit were not finished looking at the Portuguese market. Belgian international Axel Witsel joined Hulk in leaving Portugal for Russia in another transfer worth in the region of €40 million. Witsel and Hulk were now part of a Portuguese-influenced core at Zenit, joining Danny and Bruno Alves who themselves had arrived for a combined €50 million. Spalletti had returned Zenit to the summit of Russian football with back-to-back league triumphs. Now, Gazprom were looking to take the club a step further with European competitiveness.

The enormous financial outlay did not yield immediate results. Many expected Hulk's performances to join his reputation in almost transcending Russian football, but seven goals in 18 Premier League appearances was an underwhelming return, as well as one solitary Champions League strike. Of a possible 60 combined Premier League matches, Hulk and Witsel played just 37, and the former's form on the pitch translated into something uglier off it. In a 1-0 Champions League win at San Siro against Milan, Hulk was substituted in the 80th minute to the Brazilian's disgust. According to the *Daily Telegraph*, Hulk was heard arguing with Spalletti's staff after he left the pitch and would also publicly threaten to leave the club. Spalletti had shown during his time at Roma that he was not afraid to take on star names within his squad.

'Hulk can say anything he wants, but if I decide to change him during the game it means I'm not happy with his play,' he said.

'Hulk is mistaken if he thinks he should play for 90 minutes all the time. He said he wants to leave? Then, it's his choice and I can do nothing about it,' added the Italian.

It was becoming public knowledge that Hulk had not acclimatised to his new surroundings, and that his Zenit team-mates were growing increasingly frustrated with the squad's new star player. Spalletti was required to publicly cool squad tensions, with his own relationship with the player right at the very heart of the matter. Hulk demanded to leave, and whilst he and Spalletti resolved their dispute and pulled the matter back from the brink, it had rocked the Zenit ship.

The situation became farcical when Spalletti was caught in an awkward position between striker Aleksandr Kerzhakov and defender Bruno Alves. Both celebrated their birthdays with parties on the same day, with Spalletti making his case for being in harmony with his squad by stating he attended Kerzhakov's. It was publicly stated by certain members of the squad that Spalletti had not been seen at the event. That there was a clear rift in the squad, with two player parties happening at the same time and splitting loyalties, became a sub-heading in this bizarre incident. That Hulk attended Alves' party only furthered the sense that all was not well between the Brazilian, Spalletti and the rest of the team. Senior player Igor Denisov had previously demanded a pay rise to bring his wages closer to those of the newly arrived Hulk and Witsel, for which the Russian was punished by being exiled from the first team to train with the youth players. This had preceded the fiasco at San Siro by a matter of weeks, setting the scene for further blackened storm clouds to descend upon the head of Spalletti.

Their domestic form had been patchy, with the Champions League debacle distracting attention from the fact that their grip on the Premier League was loosening. Zenit operated below their usual high standards in that 2012/13 season, with a horrid run of one win in five matches in and around that night at San Siro derailing their efforts to win a third successive title. They finished second, two points behind CSKA Moscow, and a semi-final defeat to Anzhi Makhachkala in the Russian Cup resulted in Spalletti's first trophy-less season in Russia. Spalletti's excellence in his first two years at Zenit had created a sense of invincibility, especially when matched with Zenit's financial might. Cracks had appeared over the Hulk affair and the media were starting to turn on the coach, with the *Times of Malta* quoting former Zenit striker Alexander Panov as saying:

'I think Spalletti has exhausted himself at Zenit. You can see it by just looking at him, it seems he doesn't have the fire anymore.'

Images of a forlorn and dejected Spalletti in Roma colours came to the fore again. In Rome, early brilliance eventually gave way to frustration and a media battle that

Spalletti could not win. The same was beginning to happen in Russia, too. 'I am not a quitter,' responded Spalletti, and having already rejected the notion of returning to Italy due to the pressures and stresses that came with managing in Serie A, he saw his work was not finished in Russia. Zenit had to retake their title if they were to quash the unrest and speculation surrounding their coach and squad.

The club responded by recruiting experience for the next season. Anatoliy Tymoshchuk, then 34 years old, arrived from Bayern Munich as did club legend Andrey Arshavin from Arsenal for his third stint in Zenit colours. The consensus appeared to be that Zenit had laid the foundations with a lavish international transfer policy a year before, allowing them to consolidate with shrewder recruits in the following years. Regardless of who arrived, Zenit had to find a way of elevating the performances of their superstars. The most notable outgoing movement was that of Igor Denisov, who, after 11 years of service to Zenit, was sold to Anzhi following the fallout with the club over his wage demands. It was a sad way for a club stalwart to depart, and Zenit needed a brutal response to losing their Premier League title to win back public favour.

That ruthless revenge never came. Zenit snuck through their Champions League group despite having won just one match, and suffered a humiliating 4-1 defeat away at Austria Wien in the final round of matches. *ESPN* noted that the Austrians were merely the latest in a growing list of unfancied clubs to beat Spalletti in Europe during his time as Zenit coach. It would be unfair to mark Spalletti as a coach who struggled in Europe. Impressive European runs with Roma had featured a win over Real Madrid in 2007/08, and they had been unlucky to meet Sir Alex Ferguson's brilliant Manchester United side year after year. However, this pattern was an alarming one, and could easily have been grouped with the 7-1 massacre suffered by Spalletti at the hands of the great Ferguson all those years before. Gazprom's investment and international recruitment drive had surely been to not only assert dominance domestically, but also enable the Russian game to become a European force. Relinquishing the Premier League title had already weakened their hand in Russia, and despite losing just once in the first 15 matches of the league season in 2013/14, there was a palpable sense that Zenit were no longer the team Spalletti had built and coached two years before. The star names and personalities had eroded the ethos and philosophy Spalletti had brought with style and a charming grin. Now, Spalletti was being trodden over. One win in six around the turn of 2014 completely derailed Zenit's title push, with a brutal 4-2 defeat to Borussia Dortmund in the Champions League round of 16 first leg thrown into the mix. A drab 0-0 draw at home to Tom Tomsk was the final straw, and Zenit sacked Luciano Spalletti in the March of 2014.

Spalletti had always counted on the support of the Zenit board throughout the melodramas of the past two seasons, but their patience had finally worn thin. Having pumped hundreds of millions into the playing squad, the only logical solution was to relieve the coach of his duties. They got their wish as Zenit retook their title in 2014/15 in a run where the club would win six of the next nine Premier Leagues. The first seasons under Spalletti had paved the way for an era of Zenit dominance in Russia and the lavish money-spree of the third year under the Italian had set a new precedent for how the club would attack each Premier League season. Hulk remained at Zenit until 2016, outlasting Spalletti by two years, and he currently sits ninth in the list of all-time top scorers for the club (77 goals). His career of unusual moves would continue after Zenit when he joined Shanghai SIPG for a similar fee to that paid by Zenit four years before. Hulk's name is one that is often reminisced about by those who remembered his vicious left foot and brutish strength, if not for reaching the heights that many imagined he could.

Nevertheless, Hulk was the latest in a recent string of high-profile players to have gone to war with Luciano Spalletti and won, following the retrospective criticisms that had followed the coach out of the door at Roma. Perhaps it was a sign that Spalletti was not yet ready to coach a side with the superstar egos of Francesco Totti and Hulk. Many would point to Spalletti's own words on the matter, and remember his claims that he had left the pressures of coaching in Italy behind in moving to Russia. Was this butting-of-heads tendency an unfortunate coincidence of the clubs Spalletti had coached? Or was the pattern now too tangible to avoid?

* * *

Despite staying at Zenit for over four years, even longer than he had spent at either Udinese or Roma, there was an enduring sense that Luciano Spalletti had unfinished business in Italy. He would return a league-winning manager following his back-to-back successes in his first two seasons in Russia, and with further experience to increase his own coaching pedigree. After all, despite now entering his third decade in management, Spalletti still seemed like a young coach with more growing to do. Having bounced around his first five clubs on an almost yearly basis, Udinese and Roma had been his first sustained roles in Serie A. They lasted for a combined seven years, and Spalletti had changed as a tactician and as a man in that time. It is said that Spalletti had had offers of lucrative managerial jobs whilst at Zenit, including Chelsea and Tottenham Hotspur. There had also been talk of interest from Inter, which had sparked Spalletti's remarks about enjoying being free of Serie A's pressure. Now, having departed Russia and returning to Italy, Spalletti would have to choose his next role carefully.

Two years went by before Luciano Spalletti got his Serie A return. Roma had achieved successive second-place finishes under French coach Rudi Garcia, the first of which yielded an almighty 85 points that still wasn't enough to topple the all-conquering Juventus side of that decade. The squad was littered with exciting young talents, including an impressive midfield of Radja Nainggolan, Miralem Pjanić and Kevin Strootman. Such talents were offset by the experience of the ever present Daniele De Rossi and Francesco Totti, who, despite now approaching 40, remained an immovable presence even as his body slowed. There were warning signs of a team in decline, however. The second second-place finish in 2014/15 appears less impressive when one considers that they were 17 points behind champions Juventus, and that their 38 Serie A matches returned a mere 54 goals. Totti finished as the club's joint-top scorer with just eight goals.

Garcia was running out of time, having already developed a difficult working relationship with the club owners. Significant transfer incomings boosted the squad, including the permanent signing of Nainggolan (the Belgian had previously been on loan) and the loan arrivals of Mohamed Salah from Chelsea, Edin Džeko from Manchester City, Wojciech Szczęsny from Arsenal, Stephan El Shaarawy from Milan and Antonio Rüdiger from VfB Stuttgart. This was a squad being built to compete for the title, not to finish second by nearly 20 points. A disastrous autumn and winter saw Roma win just once in seven matches, drawing five. Competing with that Juventus side made such runs of form completely unacceptable and rendered any ambition of competing for the title finished. A 1-1 draw with Milan was the final act of Garcia's spell at Roma as the ownership relieved him of his duties. This would not be the last time that Rudi Garcia and Luciano Spalletti's paths would dance past each other.

As Spalletti neared the second anniversary of his Zenit sacking, Roma called to ask for him to return. Much had changed since Spalletti left six and a half years before, namely that US businessman James Pallotta was the chairman and owner. Spalletti had taken the blame for many of the failed signings of his previous spell in Rome, but under this ownership there was a clear recruitment structure that operated in tandem with the coach, rather than at their behest. Nicky Bandini wrote in *The Guardian* that Spalletti chose to sleep at Roma's Trigoria training facility upon his return in January 2016 to quickly reintegrate himself with the club and players midway through the season. Spalletti had no time to implement his unique and varied tactical ideals with this group of players and needed quick results to reignite Roma's pursuit of Champions League football.

The poor results did not disappear upon Spalletti's return with a draw at home to Hellas Verona followed by a 1-0 defeat at Juventus. Then came the new coach 'bounce' Pallotta and Roma had hoped for, with an impressive eight-match winning streak. Not only were Roma winning; they were scoring for fun. Loanees Salah and Džeko caught fire by scoring a combined 11 goals in this eight-match run, and Roma had returned to the free-flowing and inventive attacking side that Spalletti had created all those years ago. In Džeko, Spalletti also had a profile of player he had not encountered in his first Roma spell; a prolific and reliable striker. The coach's reinvention of Francesco Totti as a 'false nine' that dropped deep to influence the game more was undeniably brilliant, but it was influenced by Spalletti being without a recognised striker to field in his place. Now Spalletti had that player as well as creative outlets in Pjanić (who had been pulled back into deep central midfield by Spalletti to mimic the tempo-setting of his beloved David Pizarro), Nainggolan and Salah. This would not be the full extent of Salah's brilliance under Spalletti, either.

Despite this improvement in style and substance, a Totti-shaped cloud hung above Spalletti. The great captain and icon of Roma had missed nearly three months and 17 matches with a hamstring injury and returned a week before Spalletti's hiring. More muscle injuries plagued his comeback, before a gradual return to fitness over the last third of the season. Totti and Spalletti had maintained an amicable relationship at least to the press since their reunion, following the souring of their relationship back in 2009. Perhaps it was the form his team had found, or his need to protect a 39-year-old player on his return from injury, but Spalletti's reintegration of Totti to the playing side was careful and gradual. Of the first 12 matches of Spalletti's second spell, Totti was on the pitch for just 65 minutes and left on the substitutes' bench for eight of those matches. A 93rd-minute assist against Bologna was Totti's first telling contribution before a dramatic equaliser in a 3-3 draw at Atalanta for his first goal in the new Spalletti era. Spalletti had been sent off for dissent earlier in the match, and sources say he had been incensed at the poor performance of his side and unfurled a verbal volley upon their return to the dressing room.

It is said that Totti stood up and fought back at Spalletti, and that the pair had to be separated from a physical altercation. This was a moment seven years in the making, dating back to Spalletti's loss of control in the Roma dressing room, Totti's remarks about the coach's inability to communicate in his final weeks at Roma and his joy at Claudio Ranieri's appointment. Spalletti and James Pallotta categorically deny that there was a physical battle between the pair, and Pallotta stated that the argument was no different between him and Totti and the whole squad. An important piece of context was that Totti's contract was due to end in the summer, and speculation had become rife that Spalletti's sparing use of the captain had been to ease him out of the door. The media and fanbase was once again dividing on the issue, and Totti stepped in by releasing a statement on his website calling for unity behind the team. Spalletti sought to join his captain in his own public rallying call:

'I've had a non-existent rivalry with Totti thrust upon me. I'm pleased if he's doing what he loves. I really enjoyed Totti's message on his website. A true captain's statement.

'I need everyone in my squad, Totti included obviously. I have to make sure all the lads feel important. He is always an asset to us.' (*BBC Sport*)

Totti would find crucial form in the tail-end of the season, scoring twice in dramatic 3-2 wins against Torino and Genoa. Third place had been almost ensured some 11 weeks before as Roma never relinquished their grip on the final Champions League spot, and ended the season 13 points ahead of fourth-placed Inter. Their points tally had grown by 13, and 54 goals in 2014/15 had increased to 83 the following season; the most in Serie A. Salah, Roma's top scorer with 14 goals, was signed permanently along with Rüdiger, El Sharaawy and Džeko. To the delight of the club's fans, Totti would extend his contract by one season. It would turn out to be his and Spalletti's last in the Eternal City.

If 2015/16 was a season of readjustment for both Spalletti and Roma to each other's quirks and ways, then they could not have hoped for a stronger start to their second spell together. The coach had already improved their attacking output and turned a serially drawing side under Rudi Garcia into one that won 17 of the 22 matches Spalletti was in charge for. There were advantages to Spalletti's late arrival, namely that Roma were already knocked out of the Coppa Italia and were ruthlessly handled by Real Madrid across a two-legged round of

16 Champions League tie. This meant that the coach could focus on improving Roma's league position without the outside distractions of cup runs, and ultimately build momentum into his first full season. Roma had not won major silverware since Spalletti had led them to the second of back-to-back Coppa Italia triumphs in 2008 and his re-appointment promised a return to those brighter years. The competition's absence had been a blessing in Spalletti's first six months, but the following season would have had it marked as a potential winning opportunity.

As mentioned, Roma consolidated ahead of the 2016/17 season by making the loan signings of Salah, El Sharaawy and Rüdiger permanent, with the first and latter names offering the potential of huge future sales should their form and progression continue. Wojciech Szczęsny's loan was extended into a second season, but his stay in Rome would be disrupted by the arrival of Brazilian goalkeeper Alisson from Internacional. The 23-year-old arrived as a back-up to the Pole, but across the next two seasons Alisson would make a name for himself as one of the world's finest goalkeepers.

That season saw Spalletti become as versatile and flexible with his starting 11s and tactical ideas as at any point in his career. The 4-2-3-1 and 4-3-3 he had been wedded to remained at the core of his ideals and this squad was well-suited to them, but there were experiments with attacking wing-backs in a 3-4-2-1, and even playing without designated wingers within that system. The personnel available to Spalletti allowed this vision to unfurl as, in Bruno Peres, Alessandro Florenzi and Emerson Palmieri, he had attacking wing-backs that could offer width without compromising on creativity. The midfield was packed with creative passers and rhythm setters, and the wing-backs were allowed to maraud forward by the incredibly mobile wide centre-backs Rüdiger and Kostas Manolas.

The results were emphatic. The brilliant attacking pair of Salah and Džeko scored 15 and 29 Serie A goals respectively as Roma hit the 90-goal mark across the season. Three goals fewer were conceded, and Roma finished with seven points more than they had in their impressive recovery season a year before. Their 87 points remains their highest-ever Serie A return, and the 90 goals scored was also the highest in their history. In fact, four of Roma's six highest-scoring seasons were coached by Spalletti (2006/07, 07/08, 15/16 and now 16/17).

It still wasn't enough for Spalletti and Roma to claim their elusive Scudetto. Juventus were an unbeatable machine and their 91 points pipped *I Giallorossi* to the finish line once again. This disappointment was nothing new as Juventus would win nine consecutive titles between 2012 and 2020. The mid-2010s produced some stunning Italian sides, namely Spalletti's Roma, Napoli under Maurizio Sarri and Atalanta under Gian Piero Gasperini. All sought to elevate Serie A away from the defence-first dogma that had stuck around for decades by playing scintillating attacking football with complex tactical structures and ideas. For Atalanta, winning Serie A was never a named objective, but for Napoli and Roma their dream of being crowned champions was crushed season after season by the Old Lady. Record points tallies and goal figures were no longer enough to overthrow them.

What would it take for Luciano Spalletti to win his first Scudetto? On the surface, a season as brilliant as this would be seen as the perfect precursor for another assault on Juventus a season later. It wasn't to be, and once again the internal politics at Roma would sour Spalletti's experience. Despite extending his contract for one further season, Francesco Totti remained out of favour and started just one match in the league all season. In an interview with *Vanity Fair* years later, Totti claimed that he 'gave up' in the second half of the 2016/17 season. The relationship had broken between him and Spalletti once again. Totti's retirement was the elephant in the room, yet Roma fans were unwilling to comprehend that their icon had reached the end of a magical 25-year career. Spalletti was seen as the villain, despite the public fact that it was James Pallotta and the newly appointed sporting director Monchi that encouraged Totti to retire and assume a role in the club hierarchy.

The fiasco dominated every press conference and every match that Totti did not start. It had become the headline in a season that Roma and its fans should have been enjoying for the quality of football on display and the number of points taken. At one point, Spalletti even snapped back at a reporter that he would quit at the end of the season if Totti retired. It was a comment made in jest, but pointed to a coach who had grown tired once again of the infighting within the club. Jim Pallotta even remarked that he would not blame Spalletti for quitting at the end of the season.

Following a brilliant 4-1 win over Milan in February 2017, Spalletti was interrogated as to why he didn't start Totti. Fatigued and saddened by the line of questioning, Spalletti stated that if he could go back in time he would not have returned to Roma. There was still three months of the season to go.

28 May 2017 was dubbed 'Totti Day'. The final match of the season was seen as Totti's farewell, even if it hadn't been confirmed that he planned to retire yet. Roma needed to win to ensure their automatic progression to the Champions League without requiring a play-off, meaning that the match was not to be treated as a testimonial. For this very reason, Spalletti left Totti on the bench, at which Stadio Olimpico booed the coach's name when broadcast to the stadium prior to kick-off. This wasn't the first time, with Spalletti even being booed back in 2009 before his departure, but this felt terminal. Totti was brought on in the 54th minute to a cry of delight as Spalletti paced in the other direction and applauded. Roma won 3-2 and secured second place, and Totti had his moment to wave goodbye and read a letter of gratitude to the fans.

It would also be Spalletti's final match as Roma manager, resigning two days after Totti's farewell. Like the first time he left, Roma fans were torn by the news with many disappointed that a brilliant season had been marred by the Totti situation and Spalletti's obvious desire to leave. The football was superb, and Roma were back at the top table of Italian football. Bitterness remained over a limp Champions League exit in the play-off round to Porto, in which three Roma players were sent off, and the team's capacity to lose against the other big Serie A sides that would ultimately cost them the title. The improvement in players such as Mohamed Salah, who would be sold to Liverpool that summer and go on to become one of Europe's best players, was testament to Spalletti the coach.

Nevertheless, as nearly eight years earlier, Spalletti and Roma would part company with their relationship soured and the glorious moments overshadowed. It was the second time he had resigned from the post, yet outside of Rome the perception was very different. Where Roma fans begrudged his stubbornness and role in Totti's retirement, neutrals saw an altogether improved coach and tactician from his last time in Italy and one that had pushed the mighty Juventus all the way to the title. He would not have to leave Italy behind this time.

A mere nine days later, Luciano Spalletti was announced as the new head coach at Inter Milan. A two-year contract did not exude confidence in a long and storied spell together, but like Roma they had endured a barren trophyless spell in the midst of high managerial turnover and behind-the-scenes chaos. It was Roberto Mancini's Inter that had been the great adversaries to Spalletti's Roma in the mid-2000s, playing out a number of high-profile cup finals and competing for the Serie A title. Those days were long gone for Inter with their last trophy coming in 2010/11 under Leonardo in the year that followed a remarkable treble. In the six years since that Coppa Italia triumph, Inter had cycled through nine permanent and temporary coaches and in 2016 had sold a 70% majority share to Chinese group Suning. Like each of the top Italian clubs at the time, Inter's goal was to overthrow Juventus quickly with dust gathering on their trophy collection, but also to return to the Champions League, having last featured in the competition in 2011/12.

Inter's squad was one of the oldest in Serie A at the time. Talismanic forward Mauri Icardi was still in his prime at 25 years old, but the likes of goalkeeper Samir Handanović, Ivan Perisić and Antonio Candreva had all strayed past their peak. The summer recruitment was extensive and sought to lower the squad's average age with a series of costly swoops for talents from other Serie A clubs. Roberto Gagliardini and Alessandro Bastoni joined from Atalanta, Matías Vecino from Fiorentina and Milan Škriniar from Sampdoria, all for a combined total of over €100 million. Bastoni was the costliest arrival at €31 million despite being just 18 and having barely featured at senior level for Atalanta. Inter were getting younger and investing in potential to lay the foundations for a great side of the future. Bastoni would form a part of this, winning two Serie A titles as an Inter player in the early 2020s.

Gagliardini and Matías Vecino quickly became Spalletti's preferred midfield pairing. Spalletti had not yet found his expansive tempo-setting *regista* at Inter, so utilised the pair as a combative and mobile ball-winning screen that would press aggressively and move the ball quickly. Marcelo Brozović would become Spalletti's latest *regista* project, but in 2017/18 the Croat would rotate with the midfield pivot or further forward as a creative midfielder.

As had become customary for sides under Spalletti, Inter started the season brilliantly by winning 12 of their first 15. A 0-0 draw to Juventus turned the tide on this start and began a run of eight matches without a win that dampened any early murmurings of a title charge. The last four matches of this run all ended 1-1 as Inter's finishing touch deserted them. Spalletti was vocal in his admittance that this was a long-term project and that Inter had to leave behind the vicious cycle of hiring and firing coaches in a bid for quick success. The problem was that his was only a two-year contract, so there was not the abundance of time ahead of Spalletti to build slowly and carefully. Continuity was needed for both him and the club on and off the pitch, and a wildly inconsistent second half of the season tested that need. Inter never won more than two consecutive league matches across the first half of 2018. A thin squad was being pushed even in a season without European football (Inter also were knocked out in the Coppa Italia quarter-finals). Were it not for the extremely prolific Icardi, who finished the season on 29 goals as Serie A's joint-top scorer, Inter and Spalletti's position could have quickly become perilous. Nevertheless, Inter limped over the line on the final day to finish fourth and secure a long-awaited return to the Champions League. Spalletti had achieved his first aim, and any rumours of discontent were silenced by his contract being extended to 2021. For the first time in years, Spalletti had a stable position within a club to impose himself upon.

The Champions League had been cruel to Spalletti in the past. The dismantling at the hands of Manchester United all those years ago had wounded his reputation and a narrative had continued to build around his suitability for the competition with poor returns as Zenit coach and back at Roma. The 2018/19 season was to be Inter's grand re-entrance, having won the trophy less than a decade earlier. Excitement had to be tempered, not only by the strength of squad they possessed but also that of the group they were thrust into. It featured Barcelona, Tottenham Hotspur and PSV Eindhoven. Inter continued to bolster their squad with stars of the future, including Argentine forward Lautaro Martínez. The then-20-year-old was given significant playing time in his first season in European football, making 35 appearances in all competitions and scoring nine times as he deputised for his fellow countryman Icardi. Inter would soon become infatuated with Martínez as he would go on to win two titles and become captain and icon of the club many years in the future.

After two rounds of Champions League matches, Inter had six points to their name, having beaten Spurs and PSV, before two losses and two draws in the next four allowed them to be pipped to the second qualification spot. That would go to Spurs, who would go all the way to the final in Madrid. The promising start to the competition had given hope of reaching the latter stages, but the collapse of Inter and resurgence of Spurs laid that hope to rest. Frustration lay in that Inter merely had to better Spurs' result in the final match to progress. They drew with eliminated PSV, and Spurs drew with Barcelona. A worrying backdrop to this disappointment lay in the arrival of Giuseppe 'Beppe' Marotta as Inter's chief executive. Marotta had masterminded Juventus' decade of dominance with a string of shrewd signings including Paul Pogba, Andrea Pirlo and Paulo Dybala. Inter were recruiting one of the brightest minds in Italy, and Spalletti's position was an immediate starting point to review. The availability of Jose Mourinho and Antonio Conte loomed large over Spalletti as Inter's league form flattered to deceive. A Europa League knockout to Eintracht Frankfurt continued to frustrate, with the loss openly acknowledged by Spalletti as being the result of poor team selection. An extremely attacking side featured four wingers and forwards ahead of the base of Matías Vecino and Borja Valero, the latter of whom severely lacked the athleticism and speed to cover ground so deep.

I Nerazzurri established themselves in the top four early in the season with seven back-to-back wins through October and November, but inconsistencies crept in at the turn of the year. Inter spent 27 of 38 matchweeks in third place or higher off the back of that brilliant run of early season. They ended it in fourth place, qualifying them for the Champions League for a second season running. The club had finished fourth in successive campaigns having only once finished that high in the previous eight seasons. It would not be unfair to suggest that Spalletti had been the most successful Inter coach since Mourinho. As he had done at Roma, he had improved the style of play dramatically, and whilst Inter never realistically competed for a league title under him, they had firmly reinstated themselves back towards the top end of Serie A. The arrival of Marotta coupled with two years of forward-looking recruitment had laid the foundations of a successful Inter side of the future, and one that would win two titles in four years in the early 2020s and reach a Champions League final in 2023.

Unfortunately for Spalletti, the spectre of Antonio Conte was too much to ignore. Conte had left Chelsea in 2018 after winning the Premier League in 2017, and had become one of the two most high-profile Italian coaches in the game, alongside Carlo Ancelotti. If Inter were to win a title in the near future, they had to take the leap and bring in Conte. This meant that Conte had been publicly declared as the new coach by Inter fans before Spalletti had even left the building.

As disappointing as it was for Spalletti to be released, it felt very different from his Roma and Zenit departures. Those were tinged with acrimony and injustice, whereas his Inter spell was largely regarded as one of growth for both coach and club. Inter were in a position to challenge for a league title for the first time in nearly a decade as a result of Spalletti's groundwork and player development. Having coached Roma and Inter to an impressive level, Spalletti could now be headhunted by Italy's top clubs again. The next to come calling would change his life forever.

The Modern Napoli under
Aurelio De Laurentiis

AWARDING A new coach a one-year contract does not scream of confidence. If anything, it suggests caution and a pessimism that the incumbent might be unsuitable for the role, and that both parties can shake hands and go their separate ways should it fail. For 56-year-old Maurizio Sarri, such concerns were irrelevant.

Naples-born Sarri had been a coach since 1990 but had never played professionally. He had become a coach on a part-time basis whilst working as a banker, and eventually took up a role in football aged 30. Between then and joining Napoli in 2015, Sarri had coached 17 individual clubs, ranging from eighth-tier Stia right through to Empoli, taking the Tuscan club from Serie B into the top division in 2013/14. It was his first taste of Serie A football and it fitted the narrative of his coaching career perfectly. Sarri had taken the long route around, earning roles based on merit and the extent of his results without having a name steeped in football heritage to fall back on.

A decade before Napoli, Sarri had replaced Antonio Conte as manager at Serie B side Arezzo, two coaches who would cross paths many times during their careers yet could not be more different in their journeys to the top. Conte had been an Italian international and captain of Juventus. He bounced between lower division clubs in his early coaching career before striking gold by promoting Siena and consequently being hired by Juventus. From there, Conte would coach Italy's national team, Chelsea, Inter and Tottenham Hotspur, a repeating name on a carousel of world-class teams at the time that would almost guarantee quick results and silverware. Interestingly, Sarri would also coach Chelsea and Juventus one day but he had to wait far longer than Conte for these opportunities. Conte was 42 when he became Juventus coach; Sarri was 54 before he had even worked in Serie A.

The pair's images are starkly contrasted, too. Conte has tanned skin, cool-coloured eyes and bright teeth, and a mop of hair on top of his head. He paces maniacally on the touchline, screaming and gesticulating with every kick of the ball. A spectator could take as much entertainment from watching Conte as they would the game of football being played. By contrast, Sarri often cuts an understated figure. He reclines in his chair, sinking into the shadows as he pauses to assess his next move. His celebrations are often muted and he spends as much time discussing matters with his background staff as he does with his players. Rarely would he be seen in anything other than a club tracksuit, sleeves rolled up and occasionally a baseball cap. His expression concerned, hair tightly clipped, and a cigarette pursed on his bottom lip. As Sarri's trajectory took hold and his coaching abilities became more evident, these characteristics were championed and celebrated as a trademark. For years, they would have formed part of a narrative as to why he was an unfashionable coach, and one that would spend 23 years coaching outside of the top tier.

Having got Empoli promoted in 2013/14, Sarri secured their status by guiding them to 15th in their first season back in Serie A. This was when onlookers had begun to take notice of Maurizio Sarri, but it could easily have gone down as another difficult spell when he won none of his first ten matches as coach. The Empoli ownership stood by him, and he returned the favour by taking them to the promised land of Serie A. After then keeping the Tuscan side afloat and safe from relegation, Sarri resigned on 4 June 2015. The reasons why are unclear, although the availability of other Serie A roles such as at Sampdoria may have played a part. Just one week later, and with only one season of Serie A experience under his belt, Sarri was announced as the new head coach of Napoli, the club of the city he was born in.

Followers of Sarri's career will know that his expertise lies in coaching players, and not managing the bureaucracy that goes on above that level. His style is plain to see and it is up to the club he is employed by to give him the players he needs to thrive. Napoli responded by selling two midfield stalwarts of the Mazzarri–Benítez years in Walter Gargano and Gökhan Inler. Brazilian midfielder Allan was recruited from Udinese and Sarri sought to utilise Jorginho, who had arrived at the club over a year before without making an impact. Jorginho was deployed as the deepest of a midfield three, protected by the relentless energy and effort of Allan and further still behind club captain Marek Hamšik. The philosophy that became known as 'Sarri-ball' was only possible with a player like

Jorginho at the very heart of it. Sarri wanted his teams to control possession almost to an excessive extent, hogging it from the opponent and luring them into areas of the pitch where they didn't wish to go. The wingers stayed tight to the touchline to suck their markers out of their defensive shape and open avenues for quick vertical passes to be played. The switch between careful, considered build-up and the quick snap into a vertical, line-breaking pass would be disorientating and required total match awareness from each player to know when the opportunity was on.

Whilst it can appear ponderous at times, Sarri's sides are geared to play forwards and vertically as soon as possible. Rather than waste the ball by trying to play forward at every turn, they lie in wait for the opportune moment that they have created through carefully constructed passing triangles. Jorginho was the conduit through which those areas could be accessed. His consistency and reliability on the ball were unparalleled, and his speed of thought and commitment to channelling Napoli's system was crucial to its success, so much so that Jorginho would be Sarri's first signing at Chelsea four years later, and another play was made for him when Sarri moved to Juventus.

Off the ball, the front three of Gonzalo Higuaín, José Callejón and Lorenzo Insigne pressed aggressively and were supported by a high defensive line that squeezed the opponent deep inside their own half. If Napoli lost the ball, they were going to win it back rapidly. These requirements do not manifest overnight, and for this reason Sarri sides typically struggle at first to adjust to the coach's demands. When they finally tune to his methods, however, the results are spectacular. At a time where Serie A was still being dominated by practical and pragmatic football, Sarri represented a wholly separate style: one that was more in line with the Dutch principles of Total Football, and the revolution that stemmed from Pep Guardiola and Spain in the early 2010s. Where other coaches won by adapting to their players, Sarri made the players come to him. If they weren't of a technically sufficient level to perform, they were cast aside.

Napoli started the 2015/16 season slowly with just one win in their first four matches, but there were signs that this new Napoli would be very different to anything seen before. Two of those matches were drawn 2-2, and Sarri's first victory came in a 5-0 humbling of Lazio at the San Paolo. This was followed with a goalless draw away at Carpi, but from there Napoli would lose just one match in their next 19, spanning four months. There was a 2-1 win over Juventus, a 4-0 battering of Milan at San Siro and five-goal scorelines in wins over Frosinone and Sarri's former side Empoli. They even sat top of Serie A for six weeks before a critical defeat to Juventus in February. That result derailed Napoli's title charge and they would not win more than three successive league matches again for the rest of the season. Juventus were firmly in their dominant stride as they won nine consecutive titles throughout the 2010s, so coming second to that juggernaut in Sarri's first season and with a then-record points tally (82) was no shame. They scored the second-most goals too, with only Luciano Spalletti's third-placed Roma hitting the back of the net more times than their 80. Sarri had implemented a simply stunning style of football that had not only improved aesthetics but also yielded results. Napoli were unbeaten at home in Serie A that season and averaged over three goals per match at Stadio San Paolo. Were it not for a patchy away record, where thy lost six and scored 18 goals fewer, Sarri's Napoli could have pushed Juventus even closer.

The star of that first Sarri side was undoubtedly Gonzalo Higuaín. The Argentine had an impressive record at the club with 53 goals in his first two seasons, but he had thus far lived in the Cavani-shaped shadow that had predated his arrival. In 2015/16, Higuaín scored a remarkable 36 Serie A goals, seven more than Cavani's best return during his time in Naples. Goals came for Higuaín in a variety of ways. His micro-movements peeled him away from a defender's shadow and into space to be passed to. His finishes were a mix of brute force and deft flicks from crosses. He ran in behind the defensive line, as well as reacting to chances inside the six-yard box. No player in Serie A history had scored as many goals in one single campaign until his total was equalled by Ciro Immobile in 2019/20. The record was secured with a hat-trick against Frosinone, and Higuaín acknowledged the role of his new coach in him breaking a 56-year record: 'I thank Maurizio Sarri, absolutely, which is why after the third goal I went to hug him on the touchline. He helped me so much, he always told me what I had to do in order to improve and I listened.'

Naturally, a performance as special as this would not go unnoticed. Juventus swooped for Higuaín's signature that summer for a then-Italian record €90 million. The transfer moved quickly, with Higuaín not calling his coach to inform him of his departure. 'I feel very embittered,' Sarri said. 'I was expecting at least a phone call, be it just five minutes before he had his medicals. The lads too expected a farewell. That I know of, there was nothing.' Higuaín apologised publicly to Sarri for not calling, but stated that there was another factor at play in the swiftness of events. 'It was my decision to leave, but it was [De Laurentiis] who pushed me into making it. I'd like to thank the fans and my team-mates but not De Laurentiis. I no longer had a relationship with him; I couldn't stand another minute with him.' Aurelio De Laurentiis' open involvement with players was no secret, but the public outing delivered by Higuaín offered a peek behind the curtain at the way the president ran the club.

In the wake of losing Higuaín, De Laurentiis reinvested the significant funds on two promising 22-year-olds: Arkadiusz Milik from Ajax and Piotr Zieliński from Udinese. Milik was earmarked to be the direct replacement for the Argentine as a more typical centre-forward, but Sarri pivoted to reassign winger Dries Mertens to play as a central striker. In build, stature and style, Mertens was a total detour from the likes of Higuaín and Cavani, but he offered alternative strengths to those players. He had had bright moments in his Napoli career, including scoring the winning goal in the 2013/14 Coppa Italia Final, but Mertens had been a story of rotation and long spells on the substitutes' bench. His three seasons in Naples had produced 34 goals in 138 matches, but that tally exactly doubled in 2016/17 as he netted another 34 in that season alone. Mertens would turn 30 that year, so this reinvention into a world-class finisher and scorer formed part of an Indian summer in his career.

Mertens was neither powerful like Higuaín nor as obvious in his talents as Cavani. What he possessed was an uncanny knack for being in the right place to finish crosses with ease. His speciality finishes were a delicate flick with the outside of his boot to deflect a cross in at the near post, and an equally deft chip over the keeper when running through on goal. Such skills only looked easy as a result of Mertens' intelligence in locating space to finish. Sarri even admitted that he thought it was a shame that Mertens had found his calling at 30, and not at a younger age.

Napoli lost two fewer matches and returned four more points than they had in 2015/16, only to finish third. Spalletti's Roma and Massimiliano Allegri's Juventus pipped them to the top two as this trident formed a brief but bright triangle at the summit of Italian football. Allegri, despite being the youngest coach, was typically Juventus in his pragmatism and commitment to delivering winning football regardless of the style or appearance. Spalletti and Sarri were idealists who dreamt of their sides playing beautiful football, even if neither had won a Serie A title yet. It was another season of strong progress for Napoli, but the relationship between Sarri and Aurelio De Laurentiis was becoming strained. Back in the Champions League and into the first knockout round, Napoli were defeated 3-1 in the first-leg by defending champions Real Madrid despite taking the lead after eight minutes through Lorenzo Insigne.

After the match, De Laurentiis gave one of his famous press appearances and admonished his players and his coach. 'I don't want to get into the decisions, as those are down to the coach, so I would never dare complain about any choices,' he said. 'I might disagree with the choices, but I wouldn't dare tell anyone, even those who I should've perhaps told.' The owner and president also criticised the players for being 'un-Neapolitan' for lacking 'grit'. Napoli lost the second leg by the same score, but this time De Laurentiis praised the team for their performance and tried to cool any rumours of a rift between him and Sarri.

The fact was that De Laurentiis was an unconventional owner in that he enjoyed being front and centre of the narrative, be it positive or negative. 'His involvement has increased over time and that has coincided with how Napoli's own stature has grown', says Kaustubh Pandey, an Italian football writer. 'It increased around the Maurizio Sarri era. It does make him look like someone who basks in the glory and that glory has come Napoli's way more over the last decade. And he has never backed away from taking credit or being blunt about his criticism.'

The pinnacle of Napoli under Sarri came in 2017/18 in one of the greatest league seasons to be played by a side without winning the title. It took until matchweek 27 for Napoli to lose their second match as Sarri's beautiful handiwork destroyed all who came before it. They won all of their first eight matches in Serie A and led the league for 22 of the 38 games. Napoli finished the season on 91 points, scoring 77, conceding only 29 and losing a mere three matches. Yet, it still wasn't enough to overthrow Juventus. Even through that incredible winning run, Juventus kept close to Napoli's coat-tails and waited for a mistake or lapse in form. It came with a 4-2 loss to Roma and then a 0-0 draw with Inter that allowed Juventus to overthrow them at the top. From there, there was no hope of it being reversed. What more could Maurizio Sarri do? He had coached an elite level side that was worthy of winning at least one Scudetto during his three years, whilst also instilling a brand of football that was the envy of the rest of Italy. A return of 51 points from their first 20 matches was the fourth-best ever in Serie A. Unfortunately for them Juventus lay just a point behind, unrelenting in their pursuit of another title.

Sarri was no longer the worst-kept secret in Italian football, with Pep Guardiola describing his Napoli as one of the best teams he had ever faced. Three seasons in his home town of Naples had seen points tallies of 82, 86 and 91, and two second-placed finishes plus one in third. Chelsea acrimoniously parted company with Sarri's Arezzo predecessor (and successor, as he then replaced Sarri) Antonio Conte. The Blues had a long-standing tradition of hiring Italian coaches, and Sarri would be the latest in a line that included Gianluca Vialli, Claudio Ranieri, Carlo Ancelotti, Roberto Di Matteo and Conte. It had been widely believed that Sarri would leave, but in typical De Laurentiis style, the president landed the first blow.

Sarri claims to have turned on his television to see Carlo Ancelotti walking into De Laurentiis' film studio office. A contract dispute had rumbled on between Sarri and Napoli, with a stalemate resulting in his all-but confirmed release. De Laurentiis had gotten ahead of the narrative by hiring one of the greatest coaches of a generation to soothe any sense of injustice or sorrow amongst fans at Sarri leaving. De Laurentiis went publicly on the attack by claiming that Sarri's intentions were purely financial, and that he had wanted the coach to stay. Regardless of the mud-slinging that so often occurs once De Laurentiis is finished with a coach, Sarri had transformed a stagnating cup side into one of potential title-winning pedigree. The squad was there to challenge Juventus, and in Ancelotti they now had the man-manager to get them over the line. Or so they thought.

I Partenopei were not accustomed to hiring coaches with pedigree. That their last three appointments had been Walter Mazzarri, Rafael Benítez and Maurizio Sarri proved that Napoli was an attractive destination to grow and develop as a coach, and represented a realistic trophy-winning opportunity. Mazzarri had left for Inter, Benítez for Real Madrid and Sarri for Chelsea. At the very least, Napoli were the perfect catalyser for coaches aiming for the biggest clubs in world football. Carlo Ancelotti was different, though. The Italian had seen and won it all including three Champions League titles. When it came to pedigree in club football, few could or will ever stand shoulder-to-shoulder with Ancelotti.

His appointment made sense and was an opportunity De Laurentiis had to take. Ancelotti was available following his sacking at Bayern Munich in September 2017. Having held two of the biggest jobs in European football directly before Napoli in Real Madrid and Bayern, Ancelotti was on the search for revival. Both had ended in dismissal and the hierarchical politics that existed in both institutions had worn heavily on him. In De Laurentiis, the overarching structure at Napoli represented a simpler relationship: keep De Laurentiis happy, and he'll support you. Not necessarily a healthy working environment, but the president had developed a reputation. Working under De Laurentiis was less about politics and toeing the party line, and more a case of appeasing the one man who mattered more than any at the club.

Rather than giving Ancelotti the revival and boost he required after the chastening latter years at Real and then 15 months in Germany, Napoli caused Ancelotti further reputational damage. So stacked was his trophy cabinet, so famous was his likeable persona, and so respected was his manner that Ancelotti could endure poor seasons and disappointments like few others could. However, as at Bayern, Italian football's great eyebrow-raiser experienced a shorter-than-hoped spell in charge. His first season was a relative success as Napoli finished second for the third time in four seasons, but the gap to Juventus at the top had grown to 11 points. Indisputably the second-best side in Italy for the latter part of a decade now, second place no longer gave the same rush it once did when Sarri first reached that position.

Ancelotti is a chameleon tactician, one who adjusts his own principles according to the players he has in front of him, and he set about adjusting Sarri's template by moving away from his predecessor's 4-3-3 and changing it to a 4-4-2. Mertens and Insigne formed a dynamic and fluent front two, Callejón retreated into a wider midfield role to help in build-up and assist with defensive duties, Piotr Zieliński played as a narrow left midfielder, and Marek Hamšik was deployed as a deep-lying central midfielder rather than his accustomed creative role. The loss of Jorginho to Chelsea had reduced Napoli's infinite possession tendencies, so a midfield duo of Hamšik and Allan flanked by Zieliński and Callejón reflected Ancelotti's desire to become more dynamic and combative in midfield. Young Spanish midfielder Fabián Ruiz had joined for €30 million in the summer and was a rare breed of two-way midfielder that could offer sufficient defensive work without compromising on excellent ball-playing and press resistance. Ancelotti had the luxury of being able to field Fabián wide or as one of the central midfielders.

Part of what made Sarri's Napoli special was that they used momentum to steamroller teams week after week. Rhythm and the act of winning so repetitively drove them up the table, and delivered record points totals for the club. Under Ancelotti, Napoli never regained that same relentless routine. They never won more than four matches in a row at any stage in the 2018/19 season, and never offered a serious threat to Juventus' title credentials. There was also disappointment in the Champions League, the competition that Ancelotti had made his own and in which many imagined he would automatically increase Napoli's chances by being there. They were knocked out in the group stages, the first time in 18 years that Ancelotti had been eliminated from the competition so early.

Ancelotti had also had to adjust to a world without club captain Marek Hamšik as the Slovenian left in February 2019 to move to China. Hamšik had been at the core of every great Napoli moment over the previous 11 years and was one of the raft of De Laurentiis signings that had arrived upon Napoli's promotion to Serie A in 2007. Aside from his exceptional quality as a creative midfielder and leader, Hamšik had come to personify Napoli and Naples. His quirky appearance, dominated by an extreme mohawk, was as recognisable as any in world football even if he remained a criminally underrated player. He bid farewell to Napoli as the club's record appearance-maker with 520 matches, and had passed Diego Maradona to become their record goalscorer a few years before. Naples' streets are laden with portraits of the club's iconic players, but few can rival Hamšik for sheer quantity of dedicated tributes.

Remember Aurelio De Laurentiis' threats to force his players into a training camp during Rafael Benítez's second season? Little over four years later, the president found his opportunity to impose this punishment on the team. Napoli had slipped 11 points behind Juventus by December and sat in seventh place, with any hope of a title charge already gone. De Laurentiis ordered the playing staff to stay at the club's training headquarters for a week-long boot camp. Ancelotti did little to hide his disagreement with the measure, publicly stating that he had never believed in the *ritiro* policy. Perhaps this had an effect on the players, knowing that their coach had little time for the sanctions. Napoli's rut extended to one win in ten Serie A matches, but De Laurentiis' patience was broken after a Champions League draw at home to RB Salzburg.

The match had fallen within the week of the training camp, yet rather than return to their lock-in, the players mutinied and instead went back to their family homes. De Laurentiis felt personally insulted and betrayed, and partly blamed Ancelotti for not instilling the message in his players. Such hard-fisted tactics have never been Ancelotti's style, and he had earned a reputation for being a respected elder statesman rather than a training ground aggressor. The situation became so messy that Napoli even threatened legal action against its own players for their behaviour. De Laurentiis' son, Edo, had entered the dressing room to inform the players of their duties to report for the camp, only to be met by push-backs from senior players such as captain Lorenzo Insigne, Allan and Mertens. Edo's father Aurelio had already publicly fought with Mertens over a rumour that he would be interested in a move to China at the end of his contract that summer. 'If a player wants to be sold to China to live a life of shit for two or three years while being overpaid, that's his problem,' he said. Hardly a dignified way of honouring the contract situation of such a loyal and committed player as Mertens.

Another underlying factor was that the spine of Napoli's side was entering the final years of its contracts, including Mertens and Callejón, and both Allan and centre-back Kalidou Koulibaly had been promised a move away in the summer if the price was right. De Laurentiis had already started building the next Napoli team by bringing in young talents like Giovanni Di Lorenzo, goalkeeper Alex Meret, Fabián Ruiz and Mexican winger Hirving Lozano. Just as quickly as the allure of Ancelotti had sucked De Laurentiis in, the opportunity to move on and start afresh arrived.

Napoli qualified for the Champions League round of 16 with a win over Genk, but little over an hour later it was announced that Ancelotti had been sacked. The dismissals or releases of Mazzarri and Sarri had seen De Laurentiis go on the attack once the door had closed behind them. This time the dirty laundry had been aired before Ancelotti had even left and the training camp fiasco had made it clear that Ancelotti would not be staying in Naples for much longer. When I asked Kaustubh Pandey whether De Laurentiis' outbursts create a negative atmosphere for coaches, he said: 'It definitely does. The way Maurizio Sarri was let go was so strange, and he mentioned in an interview after joining Chelsea that Carlo Ancelotti had been appointed well before he had departed. He only knew of his exit when he switched on his TV.'

Ancelotti was succeeded by one of his former players, Gennaro Gattuso, who had most recently been in charge at Milan. Gattuso's reputation could not have been further from Ancelotti's both as a coach and as a man. Gattuso had stabilised a rocky situation at Milan with a struggling squad, but this had been the most notable work of a fledgling coaching career. He was also renowned for his aggressive and no-nonsense attitude both as a player and as a manager, so was a vast deviation from the qualities Ancelotti had been known for. Gattuso steered the Napoli ship to the end of the season in seventh place, their lowest finish since 2008/09.

It was in March of this season, 2019/20, that the global Covid-19 pandemic swept across the world and resulted in the pausing of football. It eventually restarted in the summer without the presence of fans, and much of the next season was also played out in empty stadiums as social distancing measures were enforced to prevent the spread of the disease. Despite such a poor and tumultuous season, Gattuso's Napoli managed to win the Coppa Italia at the end of the campaign. They had ground their way past Lazio and Inter without scoring more than one goal in either match, and triumphed over the old foe Juventus in the final on penalties after a 0-0 stalemate.

With most Italian clubs hunkering down in the face of the pandemic and suffering financially through the absence of fans, Napoli made the statement signing of the summer. Victor Osimhen was a 21-year-old Nigerian forward who had excelled at Lille, and De Laurentiis laid down a club-record €70 million fee to secure his services. More on the details and discrepancies of that deal later. In terms of outgoing transfers, Allan was sold to Everton where Ancelotti had become coach soon after leaving Naples, but Mertens and Koulibaly were both convinced to stay for Gattuso's first full season.

The arrival of Osimhen and the loan and subsequent sale of Arkadiusz Milik changed the way Napoli could set up. Mertens had offered a totally unique profile of centre-forward play and had perfected the role to suit the creative methods and plans of those around him. However, as Mertens was now in his 30s and played fewer and fewer matches, there was a chasm for a new breed of striker to fill. Osimhen was a polar opposite style, standing over six feet tall and bristling with angst and power. Even the great Napoli strikers Cavani and Higuaín lacked the substantial aerial presence that Osimhen now offered, and in Hirving Lozano and Lorenzo Insigne the Nigerian had highly capable crossers to deliver for him.

Osimhen showed flashes of brilliance in his first season, but unfortunately lacked the availability to truly affect Napoli's campaign. A return of ten goals and three assists in just 16 league starts was an impressive rate and demonstrated his capacity to impact matches, but Osimhen played fewer minutes in 2020/21 than 14 of his team-mates. He suffered three injuries, including a dislocated shoulder whilst on international duty with Nigeria, that kept him sidelined for over 60 days. Across the whole season, Osimhen missed 24 matches for club and country; five more than he had missed in his whole career until that point.

Much like their new record signing, Napoli struggled to find consistency and regular runs of form. A strong end to the season saw them win six and draw three of their final nine matches, but before that run-in they had broken their momentum consistently with regular defeats including five against sides in the top six. It was enough to finish fifth with a relatively high points total of 77, just one point behind Juventus, Atalanta and Champions League qualification. There was a palpable sense that a fit Osimhen for the duration of the season would have pushed Napoli into potential title contention, even if Inter dethroned Juventus with 91 points and a 12-point gap on second-placed Milan.

There continued to be European disappointment, though. Napoli topped their Europa League group only to be knocked out over two legs by Granada. Gattuso was typically irate in his review of that result, claiming: 'If an Italian team played like Granada, they'd get slaughtered!' The coach had become increasingly frustrated, like many of those before him, by the influence of Aurelio De Laurentiis. Their elimination from the Europa League had all but confirmed that Gattuso would not survive beyond the end of the season despite signing a new contract as recently as December 2020.

One of the names rumoured to be of interest to De Laurentiis was Luciano Spalletti, who had been out of work since leaving Inter in 2019. Spalletti's career had seen him on the other end of this situation numerous times.

Names of other managers were whispered as the end neared of those spells and hung over him like dark rain clouds. This time, Spalletti was the spectre. De Laurentiis' pursuit of candidates while still employing a coach were some of the worst kept secrets in Italian football. Private dinners made newspaper headlines, De Laurentiis' own barbed words aimed at his coaches fuelled debate, and searches were rarely carried out away from prying eyes. If a Napoli coach is struggling, the world knows who De Laurentiis wants as their replacement.

So at the end of the 2020/21 season, Napoli and Gattuso parted ways. Their season-and-a-half together had been much less toxic and problematic than many had envisaged followed Ancelotti's spell, and Gattuso had taken the club within a result of a Champions League return. It had been an emotionally draining season for Napoli as a result of the passing of Diego Maradona in late 2020. The Stadio San Paolo was renamed the Stadio Diego Armando Maradona, and a fourth kit was released as a tribute to mark the life of an icon as Naples wept. Gattuso was not immune to such events, and was at the very forefront of Napoli's tributes to Maradona. However, his cycle was deemed complete, and De Laurentiis turned to Luciano Spalletti for his next appointment.

This was a watershed moment in Spalletti's career. Now 62 and having already coached Roma (twice) and Inter, the Tuscan needed to make his mark at Napoli by winning his first Scudetto. To onlookers, it had been one of the mysteries of the previous decade that Spalletti had not won a league title in Italy. To those who followed the clubs he coached, many would point to adoring Spalletti's style and philosophy whilst also questioning his capacity to win the biggest matches and sustain form across an entire season.

Napoli's passionate fanbase was unconvinced by their new coach. Few could dispute Spalletti's tactical acumen or that he held a status that was superior to that of Gattuso. However, the concerns about his role in some of his great teams never winning Serie A were highly prevalent. At first, it seemed as if nothing Spalletti could do would convince the ultras that he was the right man for the job. Even winning their first eight matches of the season was insufficient evidence of Spalletti's talents, and the ultras took extreme action to make their concerns heard. The coach's Fiat Panda was broken into and stolen by a group of fans, and a banner was hung reading 'We'll give you back your Panda, as long as you leave!' The car was indeed returned after an appeal, but the steering wheel was missing. The fans had made up their minds even in the face of a record-breaking start to the campaign and Spalletti implementing a glorious brand of football that rivalled that seen under Maurizio Sarri.

On the pitch, the tide turned in the 15th matchweek and a draw against Sassuolo. Napoli remained top of the table, but this result started a rotten run of form whereby Napoli lost three in five matches including losses to lowly Spezia and Empoli at home. There was a brief return to the top after a victory over Lazio and a thrilling three-way title fight with Inter and Milan unfolded. Three more defeats before the end of the season scuppered those dreams, however, and Napoli finished third. The already disgruntled fanbase was on the verge of mutiny.

Many had predicted this sort of collapse would happen, having followed Spalletti's career to date and seeing his teams' tendencies to start incredibly well before tailing off dramatically over the winter.

If Napoli's next step, having come so close under Sarri in recent memory, was to win the Scudetto then why had they hired a coach who had never won it? There was a real sense of fury amidst the Napoli fans, and Spalletti was directly in their crosshairs. With the spine of their great team ageing and entering the final years of their contracts once again, it appeared that things would get worse before they got better.

Exploding Into Life

THE COLLAPSE of Napoli's previous season had set the wheels of discontent rolling. These wheels were not just metaphorical, either. Luciano Spalletti's Fiat Panda car had been stolen by the club ultras in October 2021. The group set one condition for the car's return: Spalletti's resignation. This was a tale that encompasses the pettiness and extroverted demonstrations that Italian fans are prone to. However, it pointed to real anger and disappointment. Milan's 2021/22 Scudetto win was a three-horse race for much of the season before Napoli's dramatic implosion opened the door for the Milanese sides to pull away by themselves.

Napoli had lost only once in their first 16 matches of that season, and were unbeaten in the league across 12 matchweeks. A draw with Sassuolo and a 2-3 away defeat to Inter ignited a dreadful run of form over the next two months that saw them win only three of their next nine Serie A fixtures, and losing three in a row at home to Atalanta, Empoli and Spezia. To many, it was Napoli doing what Napoli does; flattering to deceive early in the season before crumbling around Christmas. It was also a theme that Spalletti himself had yet to shake off, with many still considering him incapable of winning a Serie A title as a perennial nearly man. Despite leading Udinese to a then record league finish nearly 20 years earlier, and AS Roma to back-to-back Coppa Italia wins and then a record 87 points in 2016/17, the Scudetto-shaped gap in Spalletti's résumé remained.

It was the latest example of a worrying trend across Spalletti's career. His teams would start their domestic campaigns at breakneck speed, and often lead the league as Christmas and the new year approached. Then, come late winter and the turning of spring, their form and results would deteriorate as legs grew tired and Spalletti's preferred starting 11 required resting. This repeated across AS Roma, Inter, and now had come to the fore at Napoli. Could Spalletti ever find a way to sustain his brilliance across a whole season? Pragmatism had never been a word closely associated with the Tuscan and, now in his 60s, it was unlikely that his tactical or managerial style would change.

It had looked like the perfect opportunity to break both the club's and coach's hoodoo, for it was the first full season with fans in stadiums since Diego Maradona's death, and was to be the final campaign for many of the city's favourite sons. Lorenzo Insigne was Neapolitan to the core, having been born in the nearby town of Frattamaggiore and going on to make nearly 500 appearances for the Primavera and senior Napoli sides over 15 years. Dries Mertens had become an adoptee of Naples upon arriving from PSV Eindhoven in 2013/14. Nine years on, the Belgian became the club's all-time record goalscorer. Kalidou Koulibaly had been at the heart of Napoli's rise under Rafael Benítez and Maurizio Sarri, and the Senegalese centre-back went on to make over 300 appearances for *I Partenopei*. All three departed the club at the end of the 2021/22 season, with their exits having been rumoured and expected throughout the campaign. It had therefore seemed apt for three icons to bow out with a Scudetto aloft, and the anguish at such a vision never coming to pass was tangible and directed straight at the coach's door.

Football often manages to deliver perfect moments of harmony. Anniversaries of momentous occasions can collide with a team's successes and offer greater perspective and meaning. Napoli winning the 2021/22 Scudetto would have been another example: the first full season since Maradona's passing, combined with the eventual departures of their recent core of icons.

That it didn't produce the most perfect of title wins was of great frustration to the fans. Spalletti was bullish in his stance, asking for support in the face of Mertens' exit to Galatasaray: 'Some players have left and take things with them,' he said. 'Players like Ospina, Ghoulam, Koulibaly, Mertens, Insigne. They take many things. Other have arrived and bring with them new enthusiasm. More will come and bring with them even more enthusiasm. This is football, but what we cannot lose is your support and enthusiasm. That is irreplaceable, and cannot be bought.' Spalletti battled to make it through his plea as he spoke at Napoli's pre-season training camp, pausing his train of thought to demand vocal protesters to 'Shut up!' as he spoke. The atmosphere was turning quickly against a manager and president that bristled at the thought of their authority being challenged. In addition to the events of the previous season, when Spalletti's car had been stolen, it seemed like his time was running out.

The wealth of experience flooding out of the squad that summer was vast. Talented Spanish midfielder Fabián Ruiz was signed by Paris Saint-Germain after 166 appearances for the club. Koulibaly left for Chelsea with 317 Napoli appearances to his name. All-time record goalscorer Mertens headed to Turkey with Galatasaray: 397 matches played in Naples. Captain and local hero Insigne also bid farewell. After 434 matches in 12 years, Napoli's captain left to play for Major League Soccer side Toronto FC. In a matter of weeks, 1,314 matches of Napoli experience drained away, and that's without accounting for David Ospina and Faozi Ghoulam's 319 combined appearances that also left Naples that summer.

It was public knowledge that Spalletti had lobbied for both Ospina and Mertens to receive extended contracts, only for both to leave for free at the end of their existing deals. The frustrations were twofold. Not only had a swathe of club legends all left at once and left a chasm in the playing squad, but Napoli had also received very little financial recompense. The €38 million recouped from Koulibaly's sale was considerably less than the figures touted years before when Manchester City had approached to buy the Senegalese defender. Insigne and Mertens had both left for free when their contracts expired. Napoli had failed to capitalise on their assets hitting peak value and selling at the right time. They cashed in on these players too late, with each in their 30s and the transfer sums recouped now too small to take any solace from.

That summer's transfer activity did little to enthuse the fanbase. Many would have hoped for statement arrivals to alleviate the pain of losing the glut of great, beloved players that they had. Since Victor Osimhen's arrival for €70 million in 2020, Napoli had shifted their policy to targeting loan signings and promising talents from outside the top five European leagues. The purse strings were rarely loosened, with the €21 million fee paid for Matteo Politano in 2021 the only permanent transfer that summer. André-Frank Zambo Anguissa was loaned for the season from Fulham, and both Juan Jesus and Davide Marfella arrived on free transfers. On reflection, the meagre investment ahead of Spalletti's first season at Napoli make the outcome of a third-place finish more respectable than he was given credit for.

The following summer bore the same hallmarks of limited spending and thrifty loan dealings. Zambo Anguissa's transfer was made permanent following an impressive season on loan, and there were loan agreements for Tanguy Ndombélé from Spurs, Giovanni Simeone from Hellas Verona, and Giacomo Raspadori from Sassuolo. Ndombélé was a highly talented central midfielder who, along with Zambo Anguissa, could do great things in the centre of the field. Both carry the ball exceptionally, especially when receiving in their own half and facing back towards their goal. Very few can match their capacity to drop the shoulder and turn out from pressure to set their side on the attack. That Napoli now had both in their squad was a clear case of talent identification, and recruiting players specifically to fit the needs of the coach and system. For all his talent, Ndombélé had experienced a troubled spell in England, where he had arrived as

Spurs' club record signing but struggled with injuries and the physicality of the Premier League. At various points during his three years in north London, Ndombélé was publicly criticised by both Jose Mourinho and Antonio Conte. Their failures to coax the best from him was seen as a red flag, but a position as Zambo Anguissa's understudy was an interesting move for the player.

Giovanni Simeone, son of legendary Atlético Madrid manager Diego, offered depth at centre-forward. The Argentine had played in Italy since 2017 and had proven himself to be a useful goalscorer. With Osimhen's chequered injury record, an experienced back-up option was essential. The signing of Raspadori sought to address a similar need, but also provided cover across the attacking line. A diminutive and cute forward, 22-year-old Raspadori had starred in a young and vibrant Sassuolo side as a second striker and off the wing. The Italian is a strong finisher with quick reactions and a smart linking forward that knits moves together in the final third. It was uncertain whether Raspadori would be a rotation option with one of the wingers, cover for Osimhen and Simeone at centre-forward, or offer a new dynamic as a potential number 10 in a 4-2-3-1. The proposition that he was covering a range of options to Spalletti was exciting in itself.

If Zambo Anguissa had already made himself known to Napoli fans, and Simeone and Raspadori were intriguing depth options arriving on loan, then the bigger questions remained of who would replace the outgoing mainstays of the side? Which centre-back would step into Kalidou Koulibaly's enormous shoes? Who would adopt Lorenzo Insigne's position on the left wing? The answer to the first of those two questions was 25-year-old South Korean defender Kim Min-jae. Kim had enjoyed an unconventional route to Italy without spending longer than two seasons at a single club. In fact, he made his semi-professional debut at lower league South Korean side Gyeongju KHNP at 20 years old after leaving his studies at Yonsei University. Between then and joining Napoli in 2022, Kim had played for Jeonbuk Hyundai Motors in the K League, Beijing Guoan in the Chinese Super League, and Fenerbahçe in Turkey. His performances in China and Turkey piqued the interest of Premier League clubs, especially Tottenham Hotspur. Spurs twice attempted to sign Kim under managers Mourinho and Conte, and the former later revealed how hard he pushed to make the transfer happen. Speaking at a press conference in January 2023, Mourinho declared: 'I spoke to him on FaceTime and wanted to buy him at Tottenham, but Tottenham didn't help me. The player cost £10 million, Tottenham offered £5 million. A deal could be done for £7–8 million, but at that time Tottenham couldn't spend the money. I spoke to the lad two or three times via FaceTime, he really wanted to come, but he couldn't come.' (via *Football Italia*).

A short time watching Kim quickly reveals why Premier League teams were so interested, even if his experience outside of Asia was limited. At 6ft 3in, Kim is tall enough to provide an aerial threat in both penalty areas, while his speed and agility on the turn allow his sides to play with a high defensive line. Aggressive across the ground, an intelligent reader of play, and an accomplished if unspectacular passer, he is one of very few central defenders that can claim to combine so many facets of the game. For those with a keen scouting eye and an interest in football beyond the mainstream, replacing Koulibaly with Kim might have been highly endorsed. However, it bore the appearance of a huge risk to those attached and associated with Napoli. After all, this would be Kim's first experience of football in the top five European leagues, at a club competing in the Champions League and with desires of challenging for the Serie A title. It was a huge gamble, and considerable pressure to place on the shoulders of the player.

The €18 million signing of Kim was a clear example of Napoli's recruitment strategy under sporting director Cristiano Giuntoli: taking risks on rising stars that few had heard of before for low fees, rather than being pulled into excessive and costly bidding wars with fellow Italian or even European clubs for more renowned names. Whilst this perfectly explains Kim's signing, never has it been more apparent than in the recruitment of Khvicha Kvaratskhelia.

Ask a regular football fan to name a famous Georgian player, and you'd be surprised to hear more than two names. Giorgi Kinkladze endeared himself to Manchester City fans in the early 1990s as the Premier League took shape, and Kakha Kaladze had spent nine years at Milan from 2001 to 2010. As of January 2024, Georgia were ranked 77th in the FIFA World rankings and the Eronvuli Liga (Georgia's top division) sat in 46th place in the UEFA Country Coefficient rankings. One place lower than Malta, and one higher than Albania. The best Georgian talents will rarely stay within the country's system, and will instead play in Russia and seek to develop there. Very few then make it to the likes of England or Italy, let alone become household names.

Kvaratskhelia followed this very same route. Three days after turning 18, he was loaned to Lokomotiv Moscow from Georgian side Rustavi, for whom he had left Dinamo Tbilisi a year before. The young winger had impressed, so much so that Lokomotiv tried and failed to make his signing permanent. Their loss was Rubin Kazan's gain and Kvaratskhelia signed a five-year deal with the club. The wider football consciousness was beginning to notice this extremely aggressive and quick forward, with multiple outlets (including *The Guardian*) featuring Kvaratskhelia's name on lists of the most promising young players in Europe.

Cruel fate would intervene, however. Russia's invasion of Ukraine in early 2022 prompted a mass exodus of non-Russian players from their domestic league. FIFA afforded players the option to terminate their contracts, and Kvaratskhelia returned to his native Georgia. Dinamo Batumi were the beneficiaries of this situation, if only for a matter of months. In just seven weeks of Eronvuli action, Kvaratskhelia recorded eight goals and two assists. Dinamo fell three points short of the title as Dinamo Tbilisi narrowly pipped them. Kvaratskhelia's contribution was profound, as Dinamo went unbeaten in the 11 matches he featured in (and even went on to win the four matches after he eventually departed). According to *Transfermarkt*, the Georgian's market value was double that of Dinamo's squad upon arrival, and his remarkable stint captivated the nation. The winger had made his national team debut three years prior, so his name was already well known within his homeland. 'We had full stadiums in almost every city,' said Dinamo Batumi's then-coach George

uciano Spalletti takes in his new surroundings, having been appointed Napoli
ead coach in May 2021.

ries Mertens (L) and Lorenzo Insigne (R) departed Naples before the 2022/23
ason. The pair scored a combined 270 goals in 834 matches for the club.

The connection between Naples and Diego Maradona goes deeper than football. The late Argentine was the last Napoli captain to win a Serie A title.

Kim Min-jae settled quickly into life at centre-back. The South Korean's aggressive defending combined with confidence in possession was perfect for Luciano Spalletti's system.

Khvicha Kvaratskhelia introduced himself to European fans with a devastating, Maradona-esque performance in the UEFA Champions League against Liverpool.

A record-breaking start to the season allowed Luciano Spalletti to settle on a preferred side.

Giovanni Di Lorenzo missed just one Serie A match in the 2022/23 season, leading from the front as club captain.

Victor Osimhen powers a header home in a 5-1 win at home to Juventus. It was a huge statement in Napoli's title challenge.

As the Serie A title neared, Naples decorated its streets with the faces and shirts of the team.

Kvaratskhelia and Osimhen were an unstoppable pairing in attack. Kvaratskhelia was awarded Serie A's Most Valuable Player award, and Osimhen finished as the league's top scorer.

A Mathías Oliveira goal in a 1-1 draw with Salernitana caused celebrations that registered on the Richter scale.

Napoli secure the title with a draw away to Udinese. An emotional Luciano Spalletti is mobbed as the match ends and celebrations begin.

Napoli finally got their hands on the Serie A trophy, 33 years after Diego Maradona lifted it.

On the final day of the season, Spalletti's face was held aloft by Napoli fans. It turned out to be his final match as the club's head coach.

Geguchadze in an interview with the *New York Times* in 2022. Kvaratskhelia-mania had gripped Georgia, and would soon be heading west.

In the earlier mentioned *New York Times* piece written by Ivan Nechepurenko and Rory Smith, Georgian national team coach Willy Sagnol stated that his efforts to attract western interest in Kvaratskhelia were largely unfruitful. His raw and undeveloped talent, coupled with being regarded as 'unfashionable' due to his nationality, dissuaded many of those that Sagnol spoke to when Kvaratskhelia's Rubin Kazan contract ended in March 2022. Wind forward four months, and few could have imagined the scale of Kvaratskhelia's next leap.

A €10 million bid from Napoli was accepted in July 2022 to little fanfare on the Neapolitan side. Even Napoli's press release, posted on their website, appeared low key and minimal. It read: 'President Aurelio De Laurentiis is delighted to announce that SSC Napoli have signed Khvicha Kvaratskhelia. The Georgian winger, 21, joins from Dinamo Batumi on a permanent transfer.' In an age of unveiling signings with elaborate short films, this was a throwback to a time of keeping cards close to the chest. Even the club's social media remained quiet. The native Napoli X (formerly Twitter) account posted its first image of Kvaratskhelia in a Napoli shirt five days after the announcement, alongside fellow new arrival Matías Oliveira. The English account did not mention his arrival at all. Soon, it would prove that keeping things quiet was a superb move by the club. The aforementioned Oliveira, a left-back signed from Getafe, Norwegian centre-back Leo Østigard and experienced Italian goalkeeper Salvatore

Sirigu completed the Napoli squad. The overriding sentiment was that Napoli were weaker than they had been a season prior, and that Spalletti's hand had been diminished rather than strengthened. 'There was almost exclusively pessimism surrounding the club,' recalls Serie A commentator Patrick Kendrick.

It is unclear whether Kvaratskhelia had been signed as Lorenzo Insigne's replacement on the left wing. Such shoes would be difficult to fill for even the most esteemed of players, with experience in the European top five leagues to fall back on. For a 21-year-old who had not played outside of Russia or his native Georgia, it would be bordering on cruel to demand them to follow the one they called *Lorenzo Il Magnifico* in the Bay Area.

However, Kvaratskhelia was immediately at the forefront of Napoli's pre-season preparations. He started on the left in a friendly against semi-professional side Bassa Anaunia, and within 40 minutes had assisted Amir Rrahmani for Napoli's opener and scored twice himself. *La Gazzetta dello Sport* remarked that there was 'a new KK who shines in Napoli, but he is no longer Kalidou Koulibaly'. High praise, albeit against lowly opposition. Napoli went through the summer's unofficial matches unbeaten, and their new left-winger was the headline act with four goals. Many have impressed in the low-pressure settings of pre-season, before flattering to deceive once the official season started and the stakes raised. However, there was a confidence and swagger to *I Partenopei*'s number 77 that had a wounded and angry fanbase understandably excited.

Monday, 15 August 2022. Napoli's opening match of the 2022/23 Serie A season: league debuts were handed to

Kim Min-jae at centre-back and Khvicha Kvaratskhelia, and Stanislav Lobotka started as the deepest central midfielder. This was the third season of Lobotka's Napoli career and the Slovenian had yet to find his place in the starting 11. Spalletti had used him often the previous season, handing Lobotka 19 Serie A starts, but a series of muscle injuries disrupted his momentum. The 28-year-old offered everything Spalletti desired in this position; short in stature at 5ft 6in tall with a low centre of gravity, quick speed of thought and able to slip past a challenge, and the ability to receive the ball from his centre-backs and play deep in Napoli's half. Think back to Spalletti's use of David Pizarro nearly two decades before at Udinese and Roma, and you'll understand why Lobotka was soon to become a favourite of the coach.

The opposition that day were Hellas Verona, and in a sun-drenched Bentegodi Stadium, the home side took the lead through a clever set-piece routine. Napoli's zonal marking was pulled apart as an inswinging corner was met by a glancing header across the penalty area. Left-back Mário Rui had completely lost sight of Kevin Lasagna at the back post, instead fixated on the ball's movement. Lasagna side-footed home a comfortable finish to give Hellas a 29th-minute lead. However, this lasted all of eight minutes. Hirving Lozano chipped an inviting cross in from the right flank, clearly aiming for Victor Osimhen in the penalty area. Osimhen leapt, and missed, but Kvaratskhelia was following in behind the Nigerian to head in the equaliser on his debut. For all of Kvaratskhelia's obvious quality as a devastating dribbler and fierce ball-striker, an understated attribute he now brought was his height. At six foot, Napoli now had a dual aerial threat in the opposition penalty area.

A thrilling match produced seven goals. Osimhen poked home a second Napoli goal, which was cancelled out by Thomas Henry's header just after half-time. Then started the Napoli procession. Kvaratskhelia assisted Piotr Zieliński in transition with a threaded pass for the Pole to finish easily. The victory was wrapped up with stunning goals from Lobotka and substitute Matteo Politano, and the season officially opened with a 5-2 win. A 4-0 thumping of newly promoted Monza continued the heavy flow of goals, and featured yet more Kvaratskhelia brilliance. The Georgian was playing in front of his new home fans for the first time (officially), and played with the bravado and confidence of one hoping to make an impact. In the 35th minute, Kvaratskhelia received a flick-on from Zieliński out on the left, and with one touch exploded past the nearest Monza defender to move into a central location 25 yards from goal. Following one quick glance up, Kvaratskhelia whipped a stunning, curling effort past Michele Di Gregorio's dive. It is upon such moments that names are made, and the highest compliment one could pay the Georgian was that it was Insigne-like.

Not to be outshone, and clearly now the main man in Naples, Victor Osimhen put away his second of the season on the verge of half-time. Played through into space on the right, Osimhen is an unstoppable force when bearing down on goal. He held off his marker, and hammered a low shot into the bottom corner. A brilliant player at his very best. Napoli were purring, and Kvaratskhelia scored his second by jinking past two Monza players with a drop of the shoulder and lashing a left-footed drive home. Three goals in his first two Serie A matches had sent Neapolitans into excitement overdrive, so much so that they had already christened Kvaratskhelia with a nickname, 'Kvaradona'. No explanation is required as to the significance of this name, especially in Naples. A fourth goal was scored by Kim Min-jae on his home debut, and another rout was complete. Draws against Fiorentina (0-0) and Lecce (1-1) slightly tempered the jubilation that had followed the first two wins of the season. Spalletti tinkered with his starting side, and squad players such as Eljif Elmas and Tanguy Ndombélé were given opportunities. The fifth match of the Serie A season presented Napoli with their sternest test so far: an away trip to Lazio and former coach Maurizio Sarri. Like Napoli, Lazio had won two and drawn two of their opening four league matches. Unlike the visitors, however, they had already slain a giant in a 3-1 victory over Inter seven days before. As impressive as Spalletti's team had been, their fixtures had been kind and not offered a true challenge. Until now.

The task at hand became apparent within just four minutes. Felipe Anderson wriggled into space on the right wing and crossed low towards the edge of the Napoli penalty area. The defence was slow to react, and the trio of Kim Min-jae, André-Frank Zambo Anguissa and Amir Rrahmani allowed Mattia Zaccagni the time to take two touches and fire a low shot past Alex Meret. It was a sloppy goal to concede and demonstrated the work required to forge the intrinsic understanding that exists between the best defensive units. Another feature of this goal was Anderson's run, and the space afforded to him by

Kvaratskhelia and Mário Rui. This was the second goal that had come from a right-sided cross, and neither the left-winger nor left-back looked comfortable in locking down that space.

After his lightning start to life in Italy, Kvaratskhelia, Napoli's maverick number 77, continued to purr. Twice he came close to scoring, with the second a powerful shot smashing into the post after a gorgeous pirouette in the centre of the pitch. The Georgian was roaming freely, and demanding the ball at every turn. The breakthrough came via Kim, rising high at the near post to flick a header in, a second Serie A goal for the South Korean, and evidence of Napoli's added aerial threat from set pieces. The chances kept coming thereafter. Osimhen and Kvaratskhelia combined for ten shots in the match, and both hit the post. Lazio had held firm against the Georgian's relentless barrage for an hour when he eventually broke through. Again, the goal was created in the wide areas as Zambo Anguissa underlapped Matteo Politano in the right half-space. The Cameroonian's cut-back was perfect for Kvaratskhelia's run, and an emphatic finish exploded off his right boot. A late diving save from Alex Meret kept Napoli's lead intact and confirmed victory at Stadio Olimpico.

False dawns under Luciano Spalletti had occurred before. Just the previous season, Napoli had lost one and drawn only two of three of their opening 12 league matches, igniting hope of a coveted third Scudetto triumph. Nevertheless, the nature of the turnover experienced in the summer, plus the performances of his young and fearless squad, were rousing interest once again. Could Napoli be title contenders? Their attack had created enough to put four or five goals past a good Lazio side away from home, and their defence had restricted Sarri's team to just 0.3 xG (expected goals) in the match. They also had the league's, and arguably Europe's, most in-form player in Kvaratskhelia, who was named August's Player of the Month. Nobody could have predicted his impact to be so great, nor his skill set to be so well suited to the highest level. Defenders could not live with his pace and power, and goalkeepers were merely onlookers to his ball-striking capacity. With a return to the UEFA Champions League on the horizon and a meeting with Liverpool, the rest of Europe would soon get their first taste of 'Kvaradona'.

On the day of Liverpool's visit to Naples, BBC Sport published an article titled: 'Who is the Napoli winger Kvaratskhelia who's dubbed Kvaradona?' In England, the gravity of the Premier League can be so overpowering that many publications and outlets omit all mention of European football news. That is, until the Champions League presents opposition to an English side, and a necessary preview is compiled. The above question had been asked in Italy roughly a month before, and Kvaratskhelia's performances had given a very frank answer. In the dark autumn evening, with Stadio Diego Armando Maradona's lights illuminating one of the continent's great cauldrons, Napoli walked out to the Champions League anthem once more against the six-time winners.

Despite Liverpool's prestige in the competition, it was a tactical matchup that suited Spalletti's side perfectly. Liverpool's recent success domestically and in Europe had been built on the back of an incredibly high defensive line. Centre-backs Virgil van Dijk and Joe Gomez offered pace on the turn to be able to defend the space in behind them, and would catch opposition sides offside over and over again. This high-risk, high-reward defensive plan requires bravery to trust the line's positioning, but also the athleticism to turn, run and shepherd the advancing forward away from goal should the line be broken.

For Victor Osimhen, this challenge was too tempting to refuse and the Nigerian struck the post inside the first minute by running in behind Van Dijk, rounding goalkeeper Alisson, and shooting from a tight angle. Van Dijk had been Europe's outstanding centre-back for many years, but he looked a shadow of his imperious self against the brutish power and speed of Osimhen. Kvaratskhelia got his chance to run into space minutes later, and Piotr Zieliński's shot created by his pass won Napoli a penalty via a James Milner handball. Five minutes in, and Zieliński sent Alisson the wrong way from the penalty spot.

Osimhen's battle with Van Dijk continued, and the pair went toe-to-toe in a foot race in the 15th minute that resulted in the Nigerian being fouled inside the penalty box. Another penalty to Napoli. Unlike the first, Osimhen's effort was saved by Alisson to keep the score at 1-0. Napoli kept coming. Osimhen robbed Gomez deep inside Liverpool territory and found Kvaratskhelia, whose shot was cleared off the goal line. In the 31st minute, Zambo Anguissa and goalscorer Zieliński combined with a slick one-two that allowed the former to waltz into the Liverpool box and fire low into the goal. Like the other chances created thus far, it arose through Napoli pressing Liverpool's high line and streaking into the swathes of space behind Gomez and Van Dijk. Two soon became three, when Giovanni Simeone (substituted on for the injured Osimhen) side-footed home from very close range after Kvaratskhelia again dominated Gomez. In one of the season's iconic moments, an overwhelmed Simeone clutched his face in celebration and collapsed to the turf in tears. He would not have been the only one inside the Maradona to do so.

The romp continued after half-time when the brilliant Zieliński poked past Alisson having just had a first shot saved. Last year's finalists were brutalised by Spalletti's Napoli, conceding 16 shots in a whirlwind of fast, transitional attacking play. Kvaratskhelia shone again, but the contribution of Zambo Anguissa should not be forgotten. On top of scoring, Napoli's number 99 won three tackles and made five interceptions in an all-action masterclass in central midfield. Spalletti's use of Stanislav Lobotka as a *regista* was facilitated by the tenacity of Zambo Anguissa and Zieliński ahead of the Slovenian. Without their tigerish pressing and aggression, Lobotka would be exposed and often overrun. Zambo Anguissa's brilliance against Liverpool came in doing this, and then turning defence into attack with direct ball-carrying and catching Liverpool out of their defensive shape.

Luis Diaz scored for the Reds in the 49th minute to temper the jubilation, and the Colombian forced a leaping save from Alex Meret in a mildly improved second-half performance. The damage had been done, however, and the score remained 4-1 at full-time. Even in the successful years of Mertens, Insigne and Koulibaly, or even further back with Edinson Cavani, Ezequiel Lavezzi and Marek

Hamšik, few European nights could rival this. Having refused to watch Zieliński score the first penalty, Spalletti's emotions changed and moved with each passing goal. By the fourth, he bore a grin that could not hide his delight even though he was nursing a fractured collarbone that muted his celebrations. One week before, any talk of Napoli's improvement was tempered by the realism of the lowly opposition they had faced. Now they had comprehensively beaten the previous season's Champions League finalists and Lazio in the space of four days.

The only concern taken from the hammering of Liverpool was Victor Osimhen's hamstring injury. After subjecting the visitors' defence to a sobering 40 minutes, the Nigerian was forced off and would go on to miss seven matches (including those on international duty with Nigeria). Nevertheless, the momentum continued to build even in Osimhen's absence. Spezia and Rangers were dispatched without conceding, an astonishing 52 shots racked up across the two matches.

The next assignment was reigning Serie A champions Milan at San Siro. Stefano Pioli had guided *I Rossoneri* to the title just months before and they had started their defence with four wins and two draws. Napoli had won the previous two league encounters at San Siro by 1-0 scorelines, and would again have to dig deep here as Milan kept more possession and bombarded Alex Meret's goal with over 20 shots. Luciano Spalletti is not a coach to relinquish his principles. Having built a career on an ideology of possession-heavy football and organic, intricate connections between players in attacking areas, it always startles to see his sides have less of the ball than an opposition. In spite of this, Napoli ground their way to victory by playing fast on the counter-attack and taking the few chances afforded to them. Matteo Politano scored his second penalty in as many matches, which was cancelled out by Olivier Giroud's cool finish for the home side. With 12 minutes of regular time remaining, Mário Rui looked up to spot Giovanni Simeone's lurking run into the penalty area. The cross was perfect, wedged from the left with backspin to hold it in the air for Simeone's leap, and the striker's header did the rest.

He and Raspadori had been recruited to provide depth behind Osimhen and offer cover for the Nigerian in the event of injury. Raspadori had scored the late winner against Spezia, and now Simeone had chipped in with goals against Liverpool and Milan. Such options alleviated a great deal of stress for Spalletti being without his superstar striker. The coach had been absent from the touchline at San Siro following a red card in the win over Spezia for an altercation with Spezia's goalkeeper coach. His presence was felt after the match when, according to assistant manager Marco Domenichini, 'He was annoyed with a few players who didn't do what they should've done. He was happy yes, but also reproached the players for something they hadn't done.' (Via *Football Italia*)

After seven rounds of Serie A matches, Napoli sat top on 17 points and level with Atalanta while the heavyweights of Serie A were faltering. Juventus sat eighth on ten points, Inter just one place and two points ahead of them, and Napoli were sharing the top three spots with Atalanta and Udinese. Atalanta had established themselves as a brilliant attacking force since 2016 and Gian Piero

Gasperini's arrival as head coach, but few could envisage them taking the leap to becoming title contenders. Napoli had to strike and take advantage of their rivals' poor starts. A tricky run presented itself, with Torino, Ajax (twice), Bologna and AS Roma coming in the next six matches, and 19th-place Cremonese sandwiched between them. Remarkably, the Neapolitan scoring machine continued to break new ground. They put three past Torino and Bologna, four past Cremonese, and scored ten in two ties against Dutch champions Ajax.

The first of these European matches took place in Amsterdam at the Johan Cruyff Arena. After conceding early to Ghanaian forward Mohammed Kudus, Napoli fought back to score three before half-time through Raspadori, Giovanni Di Lorenzo and Zieliński. Raspadori added a second in the 47th minute before Khvicha Kvaratskhelia stroked home his first Champions League goal with a carbon copy of Zambo Anguissa's strike against Liverpool. The night belonged to Raspadori for his brace, but his 64th-minute replacement Simeone put the seal on proceedings by powering home a sixth from close range. The 6-1 scoreline was Ajax's heaviest ever defeat in European competition, and their largest since 1959/60 across all domestic football.

It was unthinkable that Napoli's attack could be thriving to this extent without Victor Osimhen. Raspadori would start matches through the middle and tease at oppositions with his deft movements and pulling deep to open space for Kvaratskhelia and Politano to exploit. Simeone was the blunt force weapon to hit tired defences and attack the box. Osimhen is one of only a handful of strikers in world football to combine both of these skill sets, so replacing him with two rotating players was the perfect option. Simeone and Raspadori both had time to score one more apiece against Cremonese and Ajax before Osimhen was reintroduced from the substitutes' bench for the European reverse fixture with the latter.

By that time, the score was already 2-1 to the home side. The first was as beautiful as any scored in a season of beautiful Napoli goals. It started as so many had done already with Hirving Lozano gathering the ball from right-back Giovanni Di Lorenzo. The captain made a bursting, underlapping run to pull away an Ajax player and leave space for Lozano to move into the half-space. The Mexican rolled a pass to Piotr Zieliński on the edge of the penalty area, and the Pole nonchalantly chipped a first-time return pass for Lozano to run on to and lob the goalkeeper with a header. This was Luciano Spalletti's footballing blueprint laid out for the world to see – overloads created by the advanced full-backs, wingers combining with central players to attack the goal, and lightning fast interchanges to cut through a defence.

The second was almost as good. Zieliński was at the heart of things again, weaving cute vertical passes to bypass the Ajax midfield. A short Kvaratskhelia backheel set Zieliński away down the left before re-finding the Georgian's run beyond. A simple pass to Raspadori was controlled and blasted into the roof of the net with goalkeeper Remko Pasveer rooted to the spot. Davy Klaassen pulled one back, but Osimhen was soon restored to his position at the top of the pitch. Penalties from 'Kvaradona' and Ajax's Steven Bergwijn were precursors to

Osimhen marking his return. Daley Blind received a soft pass inside the Ajax half and turned to play it back to his goalkeeper, with Osimhen smelling blood on the visiting captain's shoulder. Too quick and too strong for Blind, Osimhen tackled him and rolled the ball into an unguarded net. The Maradona erupted, and Osimhen charged away to the fans. Off came the shirt and his signature protective face mask. Naples' number nine was back.

In the Serie A match that followed, at home to Bologna, Osimhen was again omitted from the starting 11 as he continued his recovery. A scruffy performance ensued against one of Italy's rising young teams. Coach Thiago Motta had quickly turned Bologna from relegation fighters into European contenders with a fluid and exciting team based on versatile young players. Spalletti's team came from behind, took the lead through Lozano, and then were pegged back again by Musa Barrow's long-range strike. They had been disrupted by Bologna, and Barrow's shot squirmed beneath Alex Meret in a manner that the Italian goalkeeper will not wish to see again. Once again, the star quality of Kvaratskhelia and second-half substitute Osimhen proved too much even for Motta's impressive upstarts. A threaded pass put Osimhen between the centre-backs, and his deflected finish flew into the net to give Napoli their eighth league win of the season.

His two cameos had whetted the appetite, but a hard-fought 1-0 victory away to AS Roma was Osimhen's 'I'm here' moment. Jose Mourinho's side set themselves up to shut down any semblance of space for Napoli's creative forwards to play in. They were happy to cede possession and encamp themselves deep in their half to try and play in transition; a hallmark of Mourinho's teams in recent years. Meret was not tested once in the Napoli goal as all six of Roma's efforts were off target. The combinations and clever play in the attacking third that had blown away opponents was not clicking as a sea of crimson shirts swamped those in navy blue.

When asked how Napoli had changed from the previous season, commentator Patrick Kendrick noted a 'bolder and more direct' approach. Osimhen had always been that direct threat that could attack aerial balls, run into the channel and hold play up, or do something magical by himself. The difference was that this season, Osimhen was doing it at a consistently high level, a level that no side can protect against, nor prepare for. Chris Smalling certainly could not, as Matteo Politano hooked a hopeful pass over the top of the Roma centre-back for Osimhen to chase. Smalling is an imposing defender, taller even than Osimhen, but Napoli's number nine dismissed him from his presence with disdain. Then, bang! With the ball bouncing on the far right of the penalty area, Osimhen unleashed a brutal shot that flew into the far corner. Patrick was on commentary duty for Serie A that day, and proclaimed it 'world class'. A beautiful, brilliant goal that won Napoli a gruelling affair. It was their second at Stadio Olimpico in 2022/23 and the first time Spalletti had ever beaten Mourinho. 'Osimhen has these sudden changes of pace that only he can do,' said Spalletti to DAZN reporters after the match. 'When he gets his emotions sorted out, he will become extraordinary.' Part of Osimhen's draw is the visibility of his passion and emotion. The rage that pours from him when missing chances, ripping off the face mask and leaping into the crowd when he scores. To Napoli fans, he already was extraordinary.

Three days later, Rangers were beaten 3-0 by a changed Napoli side. Four wins from four in the competition had already confirmed their place in the next round, so Spalletti could rotate his squad. Simeone scored twice and centre-back Leo Østigard headed in his first goal for the club to maintain a perfect record in the group stages, although two missed penalties from Piotr Zieliński had made the night difficult for the Neapolitans. Four more goals followed against Sassuolo in Serie A including a hat-trick of simple finishes for Osimhen, the first two of which were supplied by Kvaratskhelia who himself scored the third.

Napoli were unrelenting across both Serie A and the Champions League, and were unbeaten from the start of the season. Their lead at the top of the table was now five points, having taken 32 from a possible 36 in 12 Serie A fixtures. Juventus' 34 points at the same stage in 2018/19 was the only case of more points being taken than Napoli after this many matches. There had been two other occasions of Napoli taking 32 points from the opening 12 matches of a season, and one of those had been the previous 2021/22 season. Whilst the rest of Europe began swooning over Italy's supposed champions elect, Napoli fans remembered how such starts had turned before. Even those that had followed Spalletti knew that such starts were not unaccustomed to the coach.

After 18 matches of the 2022/23 campaign, Napoli were finally beaten. An efficient Liverpool scored twice after the 80th minute to win 2-0 at Anfield and book their place in the Champions League round of 16. It is not unreasonable to suggest that Napoli's qualification two matchweeks prior may have lessened their drive, and *I Partenopei* never hit their brilliant best in a low-key affair on Merseyside. Their 20 goals scored across the six matches fell just five short of the all-time record, belonging to Paris Saint-Germain (25 in 2017/18). It was the fourth time in their history that they had qualified for the round of 16, and their position as group winners had made their chances of progressing again even greater as their next opponent would be drawn from the pool of second-place teams.

The next 11 days were critical to Napoli's season. They contained three Serie A matches, including a difficult trip to Bergamo to play second-placed Atalanta, and would also be the final rounds of Serie A action before the mid-season break. The 2022 FIFA World Cup in Qatar's scheduling had enforced a European-wide pause in domestic football, and Serie A wouldn't recommence until the first week of January. Continuing their momentum before the season stopped was paramount.

Atalanta are a puzzling proposition in their own stadium. Despite having historically thrived there under Gasperini and boasting one of Italian football's great atmospheres, they had struggled for consistency in recent years. The Atalanta side of 2022/23 had evolved too. The commitment to youth development and smart scouting remained, but the cavalier style had been replaced by a more pragmatic and sensible counter-attacking approach. It had served them well in what was their best-ever start to a Serie A season. This affair was top-loaded with three goals coming in the opening 35 minutes. Ademola Lookman opened proceedings with a penalty for the hosts but their lead lasted a mere four minutes. Osimhen rose in trademark style to nod a header in for his eighth goal of the Serie A season, and would also turn provider for Napoli's second. Eljif Elmas had featured in all but one of Napoli's league matches so far, but only twice had started before the match against Atalanta. The versatile North Macedonian was handed his third start due to an injury to Kvaratskhelia, and repaid Spalletti's selection by scoring the eventual winner in Bergamo. Napoli were far from their fluent best, and were fortunate not to concede again when Lookman's reactive effort hit the crossbar. It felt like a match between the league's top two sides even if neither could claim a vintage performance. Three more points extended Napoli's lead at the summit to six points and Atalanta were leapfrogged by both Milan and Lazio. 'My team is now used to playing in these fields, against these chants and the difficulties of these environments with great tranquillity, trying to bring the style of football that Napoli wants to play,' said Spalletti after the match (via *Sky Sports Italia*). The hostilities of playing away at Atalanta had not fazed his side.

With the assignment in Bergamo complete, Napoli came through two home matches unscathed before the World Cup began. Elmas continued to thrive in Kvaratskhelia's absence, scoring in a 3-2 victory over Udinese as Napoli's added squad depth continued to pay dividends. Tanguy Ndombélé had also seen an increase in playing time as Spalletti sporadically rested Piotr Zieliński and André-Frank Zambo Anguissa. The consistent switching of personnel on the right wing had occurred all season between Hirving Lozano and Matteo Politano, and at centre-back Amir Rrahmani's injury in October had been covered by Juan Jesus stepping in to partner Kim Min-jae.

In three months, the narrative surrounding Napoli's transfer business had completely changed. Napoli fan Joe Fischetti explains this: 'Lorenzo Insigne had been replaced by a Georgian kid who, despite having fabulous YouTube compilations, had only played in Georgia and Russia. Our replacement for Mertens was Osimhen, who was a club-record signing in 2021 but had missed a significant portion of his first season with injury. Koulibaly's replacement was a highly touted South Korean coming from the Turkish league. Expectations were low at the start of the season.' It was understandable that many doubted president Aurelio De Laurentiis and technical director Cristiano Giuntoli's vision in the summer.

'In hindsight, and no one was saying it at the time, the exodus was part of superb planning and team building from Giuntoli,' says Patrick Kendrick. 'David Ospina was an accomplished goalkeeper but had been holding Alex Meret back; it was the last opportunity to recoup a big fee for Kalidou Koulibaly; Fabián Ruiz had been agitating for a move away; Insigne had always been a divisive figure, perhaps unfairly, among the fans and would forever be synonymous with the 'mutiny' that spelled the end of Carlo Ancelotti. The advantage of bringing in two players from Korea and Georgia, who didn't even speak English let alone Italian, was that they seemed oblivious to the notion that Napoli couldn't win the league or that the *ambiente* (environment) was not conducive to bringing back the Scudetto.'

Few could doubt the vision now. As domestic football stopped and the World Cup started in November, Napoli were eight points clear of Milan at the top. They had dropped just four points from their 15 Serie A matches, conceded only 12 goals, and had not yet lost in the league. Their 41 points at this stage was the joint-second-best-ever start to a Serie A season, tied with Juventus in 1949/50 and two points behind the Old Lady's 2018/19 title-winning team. Both Napoli and Spalletti had been burnt before by brilliant starts that fade, but even by their standards this was something truly special. The next six weeks would feel like an eternity.

The Winter Charge

A FIRST-EVER World Cup in the Middle East began on 20 November 2022 when hosts Qatar faced Ecuador. It was the first of 64 matches, with the final taking place on 18 December between Argentina and France. Whilst many will have enjoyed the novelty of a winter World Cup, coaches of club sides watched through their fingers, nails bitten to the quick. The dread of seeing injuries picked up by their star players and the potential repercussions for their own seasons would have been too much.

Not for Luciano Spalletti. The Tuscan has always taken a relaxed approach to matters of scheduling, where others may voice their concerns in the press. Spalletti's greatest attribute has always been his work on the training ground in implementing complex tactical ideas but also in improving the players at his disposal. One only needed to see the impacts of Khvicha Kvaratskhelia and Kim Min-jae in their first seasons in a top-five European league to understand what Spalletti can do with unpolished gems. Any tempering of expectations surrounding Napoli and their runaway start to the season had been because of Spalletti and Napoli's record (both together, and apart). Both typically started campaigns like this but would stumble in the winter months when fatigue set in and other sides wised up to their tricks. Spalletti has never been a tinkerer nor great rotator of personnel. Across his career he had settled on a preferred group of 13 to 15 players, and would deploy his favoured 11 as often as he physically could. The result would be the aforementioned fatigue that would influence those players as they sought rest. This year was different as the World Cup break allowed Spalletti's squad time to recuperate.

Luckily for the coach, few of his key players featured heavily at the World Cup. Italy failed to qualify, so goalkeeper Alex Meret, captain Giovanni Di Lorenzo and forward Matteo Politano were not required to make the trip to Qatar. In fact of Napoli's favoured back four, only Kim Min-jae even played at the tournament as his South Korea made it only as far as the round of 16 stage. Piotr Zieliński's Poland and Hirving Lozano's Mexico competed in Group C together, with Zieliński's side qualifying at Mexico's expense before being knocked out at the next stage by France. André-Frank Zambo Anguissa also appeared fleetingly when Cameroon exited after three matches. All of Victor Osimhen (Nigeria), Stanislav Lobotka (Slovenia), Amir Rrahmani (Kosovo), Eljif Elmas (North Macedonia) and Khvicha Kvaratskhelia (Georgia) were absent from the World Cup. This meant that Spalletti was allowed to train with an almost full squad while others prayed for their best players to return without injury.

Such a factor could prove decisive. Among their rivals, Milan's Rafael Leao and Olivier Giroud played major roles in Portugal and France's tournaments, and Lautaro Martínez of Inter was part of the winning Argentina team. Would the physical stress of this added workload plus extended travel prove too much for Napoli's rivals?

'I wish there was always a mid-season break!' said Spalletti as he returned home to Tuscany before he regrouped with his squad (*Football Italia*). Napoli's upcoming fixtures required them to be at their sharpest with Inter, Juventus and Roma all coming in the next six matches. There was also the start of the Coppa Italia to contend with in January, and the resumption of the Champions League in mid-February. Having dominated their group and qualified as winners, Napoli were drawn against Eintracht Frankfurt in the next round. The Germans had qualified in second place behind Tottenham Hotspur in Group D, and to many this appeared like a realistically winnable tie for the Italians.

Round 16 of the Serie A season finally got under way on 4 January 2023, 53 days after Napoli's 3-2 win at home to Udinese. The match at San Siro was a turgid affair, with both sides lacking fluency and clearly low on match sharpness. Napoli held the ball well but were effectively snuffed out by Inter's three-man midfield matching up with their own. Inter's 3-5-2 was arguably the most effective shape to combat Spalletti's 4-3-3. The midfield could go man-to-man and mark their opposite numbers, and the wing-backs and wide centre-backs protect against the overloads Napoli had created in wide areas so brilliantly all season. So aggressive were Denzel Dumfries and Federico Dimarco that Napoli's full-backs were pinned back, reluctant to bomb forward at the risk of leaving themselves exposed should the ball be overturned. Napoli could not move one of their wide defenders centrally either to create midfield superiority, as that again would leave too much space for Inter's wing-backs. The result was the most comprehensive performance against the Neapolitans so far that season. Inter emerged 1-0 winners through Edin Džeko's 55th-minute header, but the score could have been more severe had Romelu Lukaku been more clinical in front of goal. Napoli were beaten for the first time in the league. Inter, now third, were still eight points adrift but cross-city rivals Milan had beaten Salernitana 2-1 to remain second and close the gap to five points.

Having been kept quiet by Inter's central defensive trio at San Siro, Victor Osimhen scored his first goal of 2023 a week later against Sampdoria. It was a goal crafted from an intrinsic understanding between passer and target as Osimhen nipped ahead of his marker to meet Mário Rui's arcing cross from the left. The Portuguese left-back does not fit the typical modern profile. Compared to Giovanni Di Lorenzo on the other side, Mário Rui is slimmer and much less athletic and explosive. His strengths are his weight of pass, particularly on the diagonal, and safety in build-up to offer Napoli's midfield a consistent passing route out of danger. His assist here was weighted perfectly for Osimhen's run, and the Nigerian did the rest.

This goal marked the start of a career-changing run for Osimhen. His 11 goals and three assists in 16 matches across Serie A and the Champions League had already shown improved consistency on his previous two seasons in Italy. However, this record would improve further over the coming two months, as Osimhen scored in each of the next nine across the two premier competitions. This relentless run placed Osimhen alongside Erling Haaland, who would break the Premier League's goal record that season, Harry Kane and Kylian Mbappé as the most prolific forwards in Europe that season. Osimhen's standing within the game had hit new heights.

Sampdoria were reduced to ten men before the half-time break, which allowed Napoli to find their rhythm and score a second through Eljif Elmas before a sterner test came their way. Juventus had steadily climbed their way to third place after a woeful start where they had won only three of their opening nine league matches. Massimiliano Allegri had faced intense pressure as a result, but also because of the nature of the performances. Allegri's pragmatic and reactive style had lost favour in the face of such dire returns. The club held firm in backing their coach, and were rewarded with a run of eight consecutive victories. This upturn in form was due to efficiency rather than Allegri deviating from his principles, as only twice did they score more than twice in a match. Crucially, Juventus did not concede once within these eight matches. They were Serie A's form team, with the tightest defence coming up against the strongest attack.

'The Juventus match in late January was iconic,' remembers Patrick Kendrick. 'Juventus were on the back of eight straight wins without conceding prior to the trip to the Maradona and had become Napoli's nearest challengers. Juventus are despised in Naples, and they were the team that had pipped Maurizio Sarri's Napoli teams to the title in the past.' The in-form visitors set up in a 3-5-2 to match up with Napoli's 4-3-3. This of course was the same shape that Inter had used to neutralise the league leaders a week prior, but Juventus deployed it in a very different manner with less convincing options at wing-back in converted winger Federico Chiesa (on his first start since a horrible cruciate ligament injury) and Filip Kostić.

The weakness in this area was exposed within 15 minutes, when Kostić failed to notice Matteo Politano's run as he attempted to close down the ball. Politano slipped in behind the left-wing-back and crossed into a dangerous area. Khvicha Kvaratskhelia swivelled a volley goalwards that was saved by goalkeeper Wojciech Szczęsny into the path of Osimhen. Napoli led 1-0 as the Maradona erupted. Their talisman whipped his arms above his head, daring the crowd to go louder still. Juventus under Allegri had become a team of moments in attacking areas where the most talented individuals were trusted (or even expected) to do something extraordinary to score rather than repeating well-rehearsed patterns of play. Ángel Di María is one such player, and the veteran forward nearly reduced the home support to silence when he clipped the crossbar five minutes later with a brilliant long-range effort. This was not the night for muted reactions, however. Politano had pulled deeper to stretch Juventus' wing-back Kostić away from the centre-backs, thus leaving room for Osimhen to and bully his way into dangerous areas. Having been spun behind by Politano, Osimhen squared for Kvaratskhelia to side-foot into the bottom corner: 2-0.

Patrick was on commentary duties for Serie A that day. 'It might just be their year! Perhaps, 33 years of hurt drifting away!' he cried following the Georgian's cool strike. Three minutes later, and all were reminded of why Napoli had not won a league title in over three decades. Di María slotted past Alex Meret to pull a goal back, following clumsy defending by Napoli on the edge of their penalty area. This was Juventus, and bursting the bubble had been their calling card. Had it not been for an extraordinary Meret save seconds before half-time, the score could easily have been 2-2 at the break. Allegri had shifted his side into a 4-3-3 shape with Chiesa moving to the left wing where he is best suited. His cross was diverted by Amir Rrahmani back towards the Napoli goal, and Meret was forced into a diving save to prevent the own goal.

Half-time allowed Luciano Spalletti to substitute Eljif Elmas on for Politano. The Italian had featured heavily in both goals, but Elmas' versatility would allow Napoli to dominate in midfield when he moved inside, but also keep a keen eye on the re-deployed Chiesa. With the tide seemingly turned in Juventus' favour, Napoli wrestled the momentum back in the 55th minute. Amir Rrahmani might have been one of Napoli's most unlikely scorers, but the Kosovan took his goal like an accomplished striker having been found by Kvaratskhelia's corner. From here on in, the Napoli juggernaut kicked into gear. Their two outstanding attackers combined again when Kvaratskhelia's cross was headed back across goalkeeper Wojciech Szczęsny for *I Partenopei*'s fourth. Osimhen peeled away in celebration, leaping atop the advertising hoardings with his arms aloft to drink in the delirium. Number five fell to substitute Elmas, and the romp was complete.

'To eviscerate Juventus in this manner, with Osimhen and Kvaratskhelia front and centre, made this a match for the ages,' Patrick tells me. Even for those Napoli fans who had resisted the urge to believe, this felt like the turning point. 'Be it due to superstitions, scars from previous seasons, Spalletti's track record or all of the above, I did not truly start believing until January,' says Joe Fischetti.

Juventus had not conceded in 770 minutes of Serie A football prior to Osimhen's opener. A further four goals later, and Allegri's side were now ten points adrift of Napoli and had also dropped to third with Milan overtaking them. As the full-time whistle blew, Allegri sped down the Maradona's tunnel only for his opposite number Spalletti to chase after him and demand a handshake. It was a symbol of the power shift experienced in Serie A that season. Spalletti, the perennial bridesmaid and 'nearly man' of *calcio* had seen Allegri lift six Scudettos (one with Milan in 2010/11 and five consecutively with Juventus between 2014 and 2019). Whilst still having played under half the season, this was Spalletti's moment to have the upper hand.

For Juventus, the ten-point gap was soon to be the least of their worries. In late January, an investigation by the FIGC (Italian Football Federation) into the club's transfer dealings found evidence of 'false accounting' and 'financial irregularities'. The investigation had uncovered examples of 'capital gains'. The transfer values of outgoing players had been questioned and scrutinised, especially when a player swap was involved as this would prove favourable in the end-of-year financial accounts. According to James Horncastle of *The Athletic*: 'They queried more than €170 million in booked transfer revenue between 2019 and 2021, alleging it had been artificially inflated.'

A fascinating sidenote to this scandal was that Napoli had themselves been investigated in the recent past for suspicious transfer activity. The deal that brought Victor

Osimhen to Naples from Lille in 2020 was declared to be between €70 and €75 million, a club record. However, four Napoli players were sent to Lille as part of the deal, and accounted for a reported €20 million of the fee. So in reality, Napoli only paid €55 million for Osimhen, with the remaining €20 million accounted for in the exchange of four players. Suspicions were aroused about whether the value of these players had been inflated, as not one of the four made a single appearance for *Les Dogues*. As Serie A reeled in the midst of the COVID-19 pandemic, the transfer faced heavy scrutiny by the authorities. The case was eventually thrown out as it became too difficult to establish the true worth of a player. The value attributed to a player being signed or sold is abstract and dictated by variables including age, length of contract, injury history, form, and the buying club's need for the player. This fluidity made it impossible to determine whether player values had been inflated.

Excellent pieces by *The Athletic* and *The Guardian* go into greater depth than this overview, but the outcome was that Juventus were penalised 15 points by the FIGC. An appeal overturned the penalty before a second hearing reduced the penalty to ten points. It nevertheless derailed Juventus' title hopes off the back of an impressive run of form, and removed the staunchest of title rivals from Napoli's path. The Old Lady had been the common denominator throughout Napoli's nearly-ran campaigns, especially during the Maurizio Sarri years. There was an argument to be made that Napoli would have preferred to have beaten Juventus in a title race without the intervention of a points penalty. However, the gap between the pair was already ten points. Few tears would be shed in Naples for the predicament of their rivals.

Away from the noise of the off-field legalities that would soon engulf Italian football (again), the hammering of Juventus highlighted one of Napoli's underrated stars. Amir Rrahmani had picked the perfect time to score his first league goal of the season when he lashed in Napoli's third on the night. Incidentally, it was the Kosovan centre-back who scored the side's very first goal of the entire campaign in the 10-0 drubbing of Bassa Anaunia in pre-season, and he had waited nearly six months for his next. Rrahmani was the perfect foil for his more eye-catching defensive partner Kim Min-jae. Kim's towering, frame-filling physique was offset by Rrahmani's slighter build. The South Korean is one of the few centre-backs that spectators would pay to watch. His speed across the ground, the ferocity with which he attacks aerial duels and the power of his tackles are a joy to behold. Rrahmani is a quieter presence, defending space rather than attacking the ball, reading the flight of crosses and not racing out to block them. Centre-backs can often be grouped into two categories. The 'dogs' are those that attack the ball, taking the initiative to the attacking side. 'Cats' prowl in the background, forcing the ball away from danger rather than actively trying to crash it off them. The 'dogs' often receive the plaudits as their actions are more obvious to the naked eye. As a 'cat', Rrahmani quietly went about his business, which in turn allowed Kim to perform his ball-winning duties.

Luciano Spalletti's coaching career in Serie A had yielded three trophies: back-to-back Coppa Italia titles between 2006 and 2008, and the 2007 Supercoppa Italiana. The first of these triumphs had come more than 15 years before the 2022/23 season, and where once these victories were Spalletti's silverware calling card, the Coppa Italia now appeared less important than the chase for the title. Napoli began their 2023 Coppa Italia with a home tie against Cremonese, and fielded an almost completely changed side from the one that took on Juventus. Goalkeeper Alex Meret was the only player to retain his place in the team as Spalletti rested his high-flying arsenal of weaponry. Rather than leave the likes of Kim, Osimhen and Zieliński on the bench, Spalletti was forced to make changes as Napoli laboured to a 2-2 draw. Cremonese were even reduced to ten men in extra time, but they held on with a staunch rearguard before eventually winning on penalties. A disappointing and surprising early exit for one of Europe's form teams, but ultimately it allowed Napoli to concentrate solely on Serie A and the Champions League.

Before their Champions League campaign restarted in Frankfurt, Napoli had a favourable run of Serie A fixtures to get through: Salernitana (15th) away, AS Roma (fifth) at the Maradona, and then Spezia (16th), Cremonese (20th) and Sassuolo (17th). That these matches were followed by two legs against Eintracht Frankfurt, Lazio, Atalanta and Milan in the next seven made it critical for Napoli to not slip up nor allow complacency to set in. Arriving at those tougher assignments with a double-digit lead intact would alleviate the pressure greatly. Napoli not only came through unscathed but also conceded just once in the five matches. That came in a 2-1 victory over Roma, and as in the October fixture at Stadio Olimpico, Spalletti's side were made to suffer for their points.

A lively opening to the match produced another classic for the Victor Osimhen scrapbook of great goals. Having scored that outrageous tight-angled thunderbolt in the reverse fixture earlier in the season, Osimhen succeeded in doing something equally spectacular. Khvicha Kvaratskhelia had been rolled into space on the left side of the penalty area and hung a cross for Osimhen to attack. Most strikers enjoy aerial crosses placed a few feet ahead of them so that they can run to meet them and generate power doing so. Osimhen's speciality is heading the cross that is stood up high above the centre-backs and landed almost on the top of his head, if not slightly behind him. His height and powerful leap can take him above most centre-backs, and force the ball high and across the goalkeeper. It's a skill that very few can do and requires outstanding physical attributes and timing to perfect. Kvaratskhelia's cross was, on this occasion, too far behind Osimhen for the striker to attack. Instead, he peeled behind his marker and brought the ball down on his chest and then on to his thigh. The ball floated downwards and Osimhen unfurled a brutal volley that launched into the roof of the net. Déjà vu had struck Roma hard, and the familiar sight of Osimhen ripping off his protective face mask and embracing Kvaratskhelia was played out again.

Napoli were heavily restricted by the home side following Osimhen's goal, if not threatened by their attack. A telling statistic was that Roma's attacking trio of Tammy Abraham, Paulo Dybala and Lorenzo Pellegrini attempted two shots combined across the match. Centre-forward

Abraham had scored 17 league goals the season before to spark debate about whether he or Osimhen was the better striker. Osimhen's two goals against Abraham's Roma in 2022/23 had seemingly put the question to rest.

Nevertheless, Roma produced chances after the second-half restart. Bryan Cristante's header from a corner forced a save from Meret in a run of four unanswered shots from the away side. Napoli were sluggish and conceded after 75 minutes when Stephan El Shaarawy nipped in behind Hirving Lozano to convert a cross at the back post.

Spalletti turned to his bench immediately and summoned his two specialist impact players in Giovanni Simeone and Giacomo Raspadori to replace Osimhen and Lozano. Nine minutes later, the coach's call was fully vindicated. Simeone was found by Piotr Zieliński just inside the penalty area, having already feigned to run in behind Roma's Chris Smalling before spinning back towards the ball. This small movement generated the space for Simeone to collect, turn and shoot past Rui Patrício. This was the Argentine's seventh goal of a season where he had embraced the role of back-up striker. Simeone had not yet started a single Serie A match for Napoli, yet was contributing with critical goals to push his side over the line. Eyebrows were raised when Spalletti removed the leading goalscorer in Serie A with the scores level, but Simeone's speed of thought and love of a winning goal rewarded his coach's bravery.

'This is a team win,' beamed Spalletti after the match. 'I have players who always deserve to play. I can't always play the same guys because I have a quality squad and it would be a loss for us to leave players like [Jack] Raspadori and [Giovanni] Simeone out in attack. I can only reiterate that this is a team win. The explosion of joy and hugs on the touchline at the end of the match are proof of the extraordinary togetherness here.' His opposite number was up to his usual tricks, declaring that Roma had 'made the stadium feel empty in an extraordinary atmosphere. We scared them.' (*Football Italia*). Roma had indeed provided two of the trickiest tests Napoli would face all season. Were it not for two moments of Victor Osimhen magic, the outcomes might have been very different, and Roma's own ambitions altogether changed.

There were more reasons to be cheerful aside from overcoming such a tough adversary. Napoli's win a week before against Salernitana, and Milan's 4-0 humbling away to Lazio, had already inflated the gap at the top to 12 points. Napoli's beating of Roma coupled with Milan's 5-2 loss to Sassuolo swelled their deficit again. It now stood at 13 points, and Napoli's 53-point haul after 20 matches sat as the fourth-best ever. The usual suspects were being cut adrift by the relentless Napoli machine. Juventus, with or without their points deduction, could not touch their attacking threat. Milan and Inter were inconsistent, with both Stefano Pioli and Simone Inzaghi never more than a poor result away from their positions being scrutinised. Even for Napoli and Luciano Spalletti this lead felt unassailable.

Routine victories against Spezia, Cremonese and Sassuolo followed. Sassuolo were one of Serie A's ambitious clubs that routinely produced exciting young sides under bright coaches. They had put five goals past

Milan at San Siro just weeks before, but were subdued by Napoli on their own turf. The league leaders' headline duo of Osimhen and Kvaratskhelia were hitting new heights, too. The pair both scored in each of these three matches to take their respective Serie A goal tallies to 18 and 10 for the season. Kvaratskhelia's opener in the 2-0 victory over Sassuolo was a throwback to his early season Champions League form and the dribbling clinics he had put on against Liverpool and Ajax. The Georgian waltzed through the middle of the Sassuolo half as if he were in a training match, gliding past outstretched legs and stroking the ball calmly into the bottom corner. Never had the 'Kvaradona' moniker felt more apt.

As for Osimhen, his goalscoring hunger had become insatiable. He had hit ten or more league goals in the five seasons going back to 2018/19, with Charleroi in Belgium, but 2022/23 was now his best-ever scoring season. Three tap-ins against Spezia and Cremonese were coupled with another ridiculous finish from the right against Sassuolo. The position was similar to his effort against Roma at Stadio Olimpico but arguably even tighter. Goalkeeper Andrea Consigli backed away, assuming that no player could ever score from such an angle. He was wrong, as the ball flew in at his near post.

Of the ten goals scored against Spezia, Cremonese and Sassuolo, Osimhen and Kvaratskhelia had contributed to nine of them. The pair had developed a rare chemistry in a very short space of time, and complimented each other's strengths perfectly. Osimhen would pull wide and run the channels, attracting multiple defenders and thus opening space for Kvaratskhelia to be found on the other side. Similarly, Kvaratskhelia was such a threat with the ball at his feet that defences would switch off from the threat of Osimhen inside the penalty area. One repeating move would see Kvaratskhelia run at the right-back and nearest midfielder, lay the ball behind for Mário Rui and the Portuguese would arc crosses towards the back post for Osimhen to leap and meet.

Mikha Gabechava is a Georgian scout for KAA Gent, and explains that the relationship between Osimhen and Kvaratskhelia is not that difficult to understand. 'I think it's not that complicated to explain why Kvaratskhelia and Osimhen formed a strong partnership on the pitch. Khvicha is a technical player who has a fantastic passing technique, which allowed him to create a lot of chances for his team-mates. At the same time, Victor has sublime finishing, great anticipation, and fantastic positioning. Therefore, these two players balanced each other very well and created a bond that turned out to be very efficient.' In an age when football can be over-analysed, dissected and labelled, the reality of two brilliant players complementing each other's strengths to form a partnership feels like a reassuring throwback.

The nature of this middle section of the 2022/23 season was that Napoli's lead kept on growing, and the likes of Inter, Roma and Milan kept losing. After matchweek 22 and Napoli's win over Sassuolo, second-place Inter and sixth-place Atalanta were separated by just six points. The three sides immediately behind Spalletti's were three points apart. Their positions changed on a weekly basis, but

Napoli continued to streak ahead. A so far unmentioned factor in their remarkable run was their luck with injuries, and consistently having their best 11 available for picking. For example, Victor Osimhen had started 16 Serie A matches in 2020/21, and 23 in 2021/22. A shoulder injury had caused him to miss three months of football in that first season in Italy, and four separate afflictions had kept him out for over 70 days the following year. A broken cheekbone sustained against Inter in November 2021 was the most notable in sidelining Osimhen for 13 domestic and international matches, and the striker still wears the prescribed protective mask to this day. This season, Osimhen had sustained just one injury; that to his hamstring in September 2022, which caused him to miss four consecutive matches. That aside, Osimhen had been fit and available for as long as Napoli had ever seen him. Kvaratskhelia too had experienced a brief injury absence before the World Cup and was seamlessly deputised for by Eljif Elmas. Amir Rrahmani's adductor issue had been Napoli's most notable injury disruption as the Kosovan spent two months out. Even then, both Leo Østigard and Juan Jesus had partnered Kim Min-jae admirably in his stead, and Napoli could carry on without trouble.

To many, the Scudetto was already Napoli's. A 15-point lead was too great a lead to possibly overturn, especially when those closest in pursuit were so erratic. With the Serie A title supposedly already decided, Napoli's assault on the second front took on greater interest. It had been unthinkable that they could dominate a league season as they had, but to potentially win the Champions League too? That was surely beyond their wildest dreams. Those in attendance at Stadio Diego Armando Maradona felt a change in atmosphere for these sacred European nights. 'The jubilation began very early in the season,' says Patrick Kendrick, 'but it was more due to the performances in the Champions League than their displays in Serie A.'

Napoli had spent four consecutive years in the Champions League between 2015 and 2019, but had since spent two years in the Europa League after finishing seventh and fifth. They had only reached the round of 16 three times in the entirety of their history before 2022/23, and now had a realistic chance at progressing to at least the quarter-finals. In their way stood Eintracht Frankfurt, a hostile away trip for any team. The Germans hosted the first leg and were met with Napoli's full might. Hirving Lozano hit the post in the 34th minute and, as the ball sped away on the rebound, Osimhen was felled in the penalty area by Aurélio Buta. Penalty awarded. Khvicha Kvaratskhelia stepped up, but his attempt was saved by Eintracht goalkeeper Kevin Trapp.

When assessing Napoli's 2022/23 campaign, their penalty record across all competitions was a glaring black mark. Six players attempted penalties: Kvaratskhelia (five), Osimhen (four), Politano (four), Zieliński (three), and Lozano and Elmas (one apiece). From 18 attempted penalties, Napoli scored just 12 with Kvaratskhelia and Osimhen missing two each. This was a strange anomaly to find in such a brilliant attacking season, and may be explained by the team not having one designated taker. Duties were rotated between players, and so the rhythm a taker acquires through taking consistent penalties could not be maintained: a possible explanation for a quirky statistic.

The visitors spent little time pondering their miss. Four minutes later, Hirving Lozano was played in by a lobbed ball over the Eintracht midfield line. The Mexican sped away into space and swung a ball across the penalty area that arced back on to Osimhen's foot. Napoli had blitzed through their opponents in transition to take the lead. The duality of Spalletti's Napoli was that they could switch between modes of attack so quickly. Their quick and short build-up would tease away at an opponent's press and progress through the thirds with clever interchanges between players.

This goal, however, showed their willingness to play the long ball when needed and exploit space in the opponent's half.

Players like Lozano, Osimhen and Kvaratskhelia are so fast and direct that a defence will always be wary of playing too high and leaving space behind. Eintracht paid the price for doing so, and were dealt a second blow in quick succession. Again it was Lozano supplying Osimhen, but this goal was created by Napoli's aggressive press straight from kick-off. As Eintracht rolled the ball back, a clear 2-4 pressing structure emerged. Here, Zieliński joined the front three to pressure the ball player. In rolling the ball back to the defence, Eintracht invited Osimhen to chase and close down the central centre-back (now in control of the ball). The player had two options. He could play to either of his wide centre-backs, but they were being shadowed by both Kvaratskhelia to the left and Lozano to the right. The alternative was to play a long ball, alleviate the pressure momentarily but likely concede possession to Napoli further up the field.

Kristijan Jakić was the player in possession, and elected to play to his left-sided centre-back. This acted as a trigger for Lozano to advance, curving his run to both pressure the ball and also cut off the passing lane to the left-sided wing-back. Lozano was too quick and pinched the ball back to square for Osimhen once again. After a moment of jubilation, the assistant referee's flag was raised as Osimhen had strayed offside. There was no goal to show for this execution, but a moral win could be taken.

Napoli's superiority was reinforced when Eintracht's Randal Kolo Muani was sent off for a dangerous tackle on André-Frank Zambo Anguissa in the 58th minute, and victory was sealed by Giovanni Di Lorenzo shortly after the hour mark. A perfect pass-and-move goal was finished by the captain with the ball having started deep on the left side and working its way through Zambo Anguissa, Zieliński and Kvaratskhelia with a series of flicks and passes. The captain moved inside on the right and clipped a left-footed finish into the far corner. They had scored twice from an xG of 2.8 (propped up by the earlier missed penalty) and had restricted the Germans to just 0.4 of their own. It had been a lesson in controlling a match through sustained ball possession (69% to Eintracht's 31%, and 666 completed passes to 247) whilst knowing when to go direct and utilise the straight line speed of their attacking players. This was Luciano Spalletti's Napoli at their purring best in Europe.

Before they could play the second leg at the Maradona, Napoli had to face Empoli, Lazio and Atalanta in Serie A. Only one change was made to the side that triumphed in Frankfurt as Mário Rui replaced Mathías Oliveira at left-back. Against Empoli, the Portuguese became Napoli's first (and only) player to be sent off in Serie A that season to taint a professional performance in Florence. An own goal and Osimhen's 19th Serie A goal of the season in just his 20th appearance had put Napoli 2-0 up, but Mário Rui's impetuous kick out at Francesco Caputo sullied the victory.

Until that point, Napoli's number six had had an outstanding match. No player completed more than his 71 passes, his seven progressive passes nor the ten passes into the final third he attempted from left-back. He had become an integral cog to the Spalletti tactical machine by inverting to help overload the midfield and also offer a crossing option. Kvaratskhelia's dynamic movement would stretch defences and pull them out of position, which in turn allowed Mário Rui the time to pick his head up and whip crosses in. The reliable Oliveira was an able deputy and offered a more conventional left-back option as a physical runner, and the pair would go on to share possession of the role across the season. The Uruguayan was returned to the starting 11 for the visit of Lazio to the Maradona a week later in an otherwise full-strength Napoli side.

Maurizio Sarri had changed significantly since his days on the Maradona's touchline. His side had been based around his relentless ideology of playing his way, built around a core of brilliant players: ball retention at any cost, slow and sometimes ponderous build-up before an explosive switch of play to free his attack. His stint at Chelsea had begun to dent this obsession, and his short-lived but title-winning season with Juventus forced him further from the dogma. Now at Lazio, with a thinner and less technical squad than any of those mentioned, Sarri had become more of a pragmatist. By the end of the campaign, Lazio averaged the eighth-highest possession figure in Serie A (52.1%), but attempted the fourth-most tackles in the attacking third (87 across the season). The patient possession had been replaced with a willingness to sit back against the better sides and create chances by winning the ball high.

This was clearly the gameplan to take down Napoli in March 2023. A low-quality affair yielded few chances for either side; only three of the attempted 19 shots were on target. The deadlock was eventually broken by a moment of magic, and not by a player in Napoli blue. Matías Vecino stood 20 yards from goal and waited for a bouncing ball to fall before him. He paused, took a step, and struck cleanly through to send it skidding and bouncing over Alex Meret's dive. Napoli were behind at home. A late rally featured Osimhen heading against the crossbar and Kim's header being saved off the goal line by Ivan Provedel, but Lazio also hit the woodwork via Sergej Milinković-Savić's free kick.

For the first time since 10 April 2022, 15 home matches ago, Napoli were beaten in a Serie A match at Stadio Diego Armando Maradona. They had only failed to win at home once in the league all season (the 1-1 draw with Lecce in August), and their eight-match winning run had ended. Sarri's adapted pragmatism had prevailed at the stadium he once called his own. Their pursuit of a top-four spot had been strengthened as they now sat third, a point above Milan and two behind Inter. Napoli, meanwhile, had had their 18-point lead cut to 15. Interestingly,

Lazio's defeat of Napoli meant that this was no longer *I Partenopei*'s best-ever points tally after 25 matches. They now sat sixth overall on 65 points, one point behind the 66 points attained at the same stage in 2017/18. The Napoli coach that season? Maurizio Sarri.

Defeat had hardly been a disaster for Napoli and Spalletti. It was only their second defeat of the league season and third overall, and the 15-point lead they had over Inter was already deemed insurmountable by many pundits. Nevertheless, it was essential that complacency wasn't allowed to set in. A lead of 15 points can quickly become 12, and then nine, with just a couple of bad results. With Atalanta and Milan both to play in the next four, Napoli had to snap back into winning ways. Against Atalanta, they did just this and found their spark after the disappointment of the performance against Lazio.

Khvicha Kvaratskhelia had not scored or assisted against Empoli or Lazio, making it just the third time all season he had gone two matches without contributing to a goal. The Georgian's early explosion had matured into something far greater. He already had ten goals and nine assists in the league, leading Serie A for assists in the process, and had just collected his second Player of the Month award. Kvaratskhelia was already being discussed as Serie A's best player after 21 appearances in the competition. That his goal against Atalanta might not even make the cut of the best five efforts from Kvaratskhelia in 2022/23 is testament to the standard he had already produced.

The construction was textbook Napoli. Zambo Anguissa won the ball on the halfway line, just to the right of centre, and Osimhen accelerated from a standing start to gather and run at the Atalanta defence. A simple pass across the edge of the penalty area found Kvaratskhelia in the left half-space with Atalanta's Rafael Tolói for company. Kvaratskhelia took a touch to the right before dragging the ball sharply back to the left, twisting the Atalanta captain around so that he was facing the wrong way. Two other white shirts slid across, hoping to block a shot that never came. Like a cat toying with a ball on a string, Kvaratskhelia caused Tolói to contort back the other way with another touch back to the right to complete the zig-zag.

The freeze-frame before 'Kvaradona' shoots is iconic. Two Atalanta shirts between him and the goal, Tolói lunging across, and four other opponents in close proximity. Seven defenders and the goalkeeper, with not another blue shirt in sight. It could easily have been a still image of Maradona in his untouchable prime. The finishing touch was brutal, skimming off the head of Giorgio Scalvini and nearly tearing the net from the goal. With Amir Rrahmani completing the scoreline, Napoli swiftly eradicated any doubts formed from their loss to Lazio. Their ruthless streak was back, dominating a side that has a history of taking results away from the Maradona. As had so often been the case in 2022/23, Kvaratskhelia took the headlines for his wizardry, but beneath the bonnet there lay another superb performance.

Stanislav Lobotka had been quietly excellent all season and featured in every single match in both Serie A and the Champions League. Two of the most unconvincing performances of the campaign were the 1-1 draw with

Lecce and the 1-0 victory at home to Spezia in August and September respectively. These two matches were the only two that Lobotka had not started for Napoli that season. Lobotka was tailor-made for the *regista* role demanded of him by Spalletti. The Slovenian would drop between the centre-backs to aid build-up, sometimes even from goal kicks. He was very difficult to dispossess as his slight frame allows him to roll away from tackles and get Napoli attacks going. Above all, Lobotka is an exceptionally safe passer and would not concede possession in dangerous areas. Against Atalanta, Lobotka completed 87 of his attempted 90 passes, and each of his six attempted long passes found a team-mate. No player in the match made more passes into the final third (eight) as Lobotka switched between recycling the ball and moving it quickly around the midfield, to progressing it into more dangerous areas. It is upon such solid foundations that the more expressive individuals around him can flourish, but Lobotka himself is a joy to watch.

The twitchiness that had followed the loss to Lazio had not been lost on Luciano Spalletti. Call it sensitivity or awareness, Spalletti has always picked up on changes in the atmosphere around his sides. It could be the effect of his spells at Roma, and the tidal change that had caused fans to whistle and direct their anger towards him surrounding Francesco Totti's retirement. Even at Napoli he had seen first-hand the speed with which the fanbase can castigate their coach. Despite recording one of their best-ever starts to a campaign and eventually finishing third, the ultras were vociferous in blaming Spalletti for not winning their long-awaited Scudetto.

With his record of fading title charges, the 1-0 defeat to Lazio had caused a mild sense of unease. It couldn't happen again, could it? Spalletti had picked up on this, and acknowledged it after the win over Atalanta. 'Here, we are not satisfied with finishing third. Last year they [the fans] told us everything and now we have to win.' Spalletti continued: 'We were coming off a defeat and once again Napoli reacted as a great team. After the match we lost, many rushed on us. We have an exceptional fan-base behind us.' (*Get Italian Football News*). That exceptional support was about to be tested by something more than just football.

In the hours that preceded the arrival of Eintracht Frankfurt in Naples, the city streets were a warzone. The Eintracht ultras and travelling fans have a reputation for causing scenes in opposition cities, but this was something altogether different. Missiles were thrown through shop windows, cars set on fire, and brutal clashes took place between police and the fans. It is said that the Eintracht group were assisted by Atalanta ultras that had travelled down to Naples from Bergamo. Bad blood runs between Napoli and Atalanta, going back to the 1980s when the two sets of supporters attacked each other multiple times. For the match between the pair just four days earlier, Atalanta ultras had been banned from attending for this very reason.

This group of ultras share a friendship with Eintracht Frankfurt due to their mostly left-leaning politics, and took the opportunity to partake in the scenes of 14 March 2023. Security had banned any German-born fans from entering the stadium for the Champions League tie. This order was then adjusted on appeal to only ban Frankfurt-born fans from attending in an effort to quash any potential violence between supporter groups. According to *Football Italia*, it is alleged that Atalanta fans helped their Eintracht counterparts to buy tickets for the match and therefore not flag as being German-born ticketholders. The 400 Eintracht ultras arrived in Naples alongside the Atalanta group having travelled from Bergamo, and were met by an estimated 800 Neapolitan police, a distasteful and frightening precursor to an historic night for Napoli.

The match that followed was a procession. Napoli, already 2-0 up from the first leg, scored three times in 20 minutes to book their place in the Champions League quarter-finals for the first time. Osimhen was sublime, leaping into the air to loop a header into the top corner for the first and stretching to tap home the second. 'Europe, beware!' warned TNT Sports' commentary. Napoli's status as a dark horse for European club football's most prestigious title was gaining traction. If they were to win their first league title since the days of Diego Maradona, could their first European trophy since the 1988/89 UEFA Cup that was hoisted by their greatest-ever player be possible too? Of the remaining eight teams in the competition, only they and Manchester City had never won it. Pep Guardiola's side were favourites too, so Napoli were the outsiders even if they were runaway Serie A leaders.

Their path to the latter stages took an intriguing turn as the quarter-final draws took place. Many would have prayed to avoid the likes of City, Bayern Munich and Real Madrid. Their opponents could be found much closer to home, as Spalletti's side were drawn against Milan in an all-Italian quarter-final. They sat 20 points and three places apart in the league but Milan's heritage in the Champions League was bettered only by Real Madrid. The narratives were fascinating. Luciano Spalletti's league-leading attacking machine against the seven-time Champions League winners. In the words of Fabio Cappello, *calcio* was back.

Goduria

'DESCRIBE NAPOLI'S 2022/23 season in one word.' This is what I ask of Serie A commentator Patrick Kendrick. Patrick had become synonymous with Napoli's title charge as I watched and rewatched Spalletti's side go from exciting underdogs to carving out one of the greatest seasons in Serie A history both statistically and aesthetically. So many of the great moments – Victor Osimhen's pair of outrageous goals against Roma home and away, Khvicha Kvaratskhelia's weaving and winding Maradona-esque strike to beat Atalanta, the 5-1 humbling of Juventus – had been accompanied by his commentary. It felt appropriate to ask what his own personal sentiment was at the end of it all. 'Sorry for being pretentious, but the word I'm going for is *goduria*. It's essentially "joy" but has connotations of really savouring something.'

Even in the early spring as Napoli advanced past Eintracht Frankfurt in the Champions League and established a 15-point lead in Serie A, Naples had begun to enjoy and savour the glory on its horizon. It is an expressive and sensually stimulating city, from its noises and smells to its commemorative shrines and murals. Naples decorates itself on a daily basis, let alone when its beloved Napoli are about to achieve something historic. With the best part of three months remaining of the season, Naples had crowned Serie A's winners, and effectively declared its 33-year wait for a Scudetto to be over. Blue and white streamers fluttered across narrow side streets, connecting the shuttered windows above.

One now-iconic stepped street hung 11 Napoli shirts in a 4-3-3 formation from the aforementioned streamers, with the names of the 2022/23 players on their backs. They read: Alex Meret, Giovanni Di Lorenzo, Amir Rrahmani, Kim Min-jae, Mário Rui, Stanislav Lobotka, André-Frank Zambo Anguissa, Piotr Zieliński, Hirving Lozano, Victor Osimhen, Khvicha Kvaratskhelia. There are of course others that had also played their part. Matteo Politano, Eljif Elmas, Tanguy Ndombélé, Giovanni Simeone, Giacomo Raspadori, Juan Jesus, Mathías Oliveira and Leo Østigard had all made crucial contributions. However, the aesthetic of Luciano Spalletti's 4-3-3 with his favoured starting 11 was something to behold. Turn on to another street and you would find the same players honoured, but this time with their faces painted atop the bodies of cherubs. This is Naples, after all. Street after street, wall after wall. The faces, shirts and names were everywhere.

They are not the only ones, of course. It has become a well-trodden pilgrimage for the football obsessive to visit Naples' Spanish quarter and head for Via Emanuele de Deo. There stands a ten-storey painting of Diego Armando Maradona, complete in 1989/90 Napoli kit; the last time the city had celebrated a league title. Much like Maradona's presence in the city, his depiction here looms large over the crowds that congregate beneath it. It was the site of great mourning in November 2020 when the Argentine's death was announced.

Maradona's legacy is riddled with dualities. The charming genius with a troubled personal life. One of the best to ever play the game, yet often remembered best for his infamous 'Hand of God' incident (at least on English shores, anyway). A boy who encompassed the spirit of the Argentine *pibe*, yet also defined the character and culture of a city over 11,000 km away. His passing triggered an outpouring of grief across two continents. Naples is a city that expresses its emotions visually. Murals and shrines are dotted throughout, commemorating the departed and offering a site of reflection and grief for those affected. Maradona has many dedicated to his memory across the Spanish Quarter to accompany the murals and swathes of brickwork painted with his image.

Recent years had seen the Sarri era of Napoli players join Maradona on street walls. Marek Hamšik, Lorenzo Insigne, Dries Mertens, Edinson Cavani, Kalidou Koulibaly, to name a few: heroes anointed for their efforts at restoring Napoli to the top of Italian football. The class of 2022/23 were different. For the undoubted superstar talent that team possessed in Osimhen, Kvaratskhelia and Kim for example, they were to be celebrated as a collective. Their shirts were hung in formation, each honoured with a spray-painted section of concrete. Perhaps this was the product of being the first Napoli team since Maradona to win the Scudetto, or maybe it reflected the style and philosophy Luciano Spalletti had curated. A squad in perfect harmony with itself, which functioned to maximise its strengths and protect its weaknesses. Being the idealist and romantic that he is, one imagines that this detail was not lost on Spalletti.

There were still 12 matches of the league season to go, plus a potential five more in the Champions League. Naples had decided, however, that the title was theirs. Even the most cynical of fans would struggle to doubt the gravity of an 18-point lead after 26 matches. The bunting was hung, the schedule marked by which match could potentially see them officially crowned. One in particular, the away trip to Juventus in matchweek 31, looked especially appealing. The mere thought of being crowned champions on the pitch of their long-time tormenters was tantalising. Scudetto fever had completely consumed Naples, something that surprised Patrick Kendrick. 'The sight of Scudetto merchandise beginning to appear in the city, months before the title was sealed, was a tangible sign of how expectant the fans had become. For a city as superstitious as Naples, that remains quite a legacy.'

The title was not sealed, nor the legacy written, however. The first of the final 12 Serie A matches, which had taken on the appearance of a countdown, was away to Torino. A tricky proposition at home with an appetite for downing the league's best sides, *Il Toro* went behind within the first ten minutes. Khvicha Kvaratskhelia's corner found a rampant Victor Osimhen and the Nigerian nodded in his 20th Serie A goal of the season. Scoring had become a habit for Osimhen; the greatest trait a striker can possess. Nevertheless, it was a team-mate at the other end of the pitch that perhaps deserved even greater plaudits for their role in this match.

Alex Meret had experienced a rather quiet season. So petrified were the opposition of attacking Napoli, and so brilliant were the defence in front of him, that Meret was largely an onlooker to proceedings. His distribution and comfort on the ball were invaluable to Spalletti's aspirations to build up from deep, but his work as a shot-stopper had been limited. Conceding only 16 goals in 26 league matches is the workload goalkeepers dream about. When called upon, Meret continued to be a reliable presence, and his save to prevent a Torino equaliser was breathtaking. Samuele Ricci found space 20 yards from goal and fizzed an effort through a crowd and into Meret's midriff. It was a comfortable save, but the power of the shot caused the ball to drop and backspin dangerously towards the goal line. Meret had dropped to his haunches upon saving the shot but leapt across to save the rebound from being poked in. The follow-up shot was prodded against the post via a touch from Meret's hand.

Torino piled on the pressure, attacking Napoli as few had throughout the campaign. They took six unanswered shots in the space of ten minutes as Napoli struggled to wrestle control of the match. Their pressure amounted to little, as Kvaratskhelia was brought down by a reckless swipe from behind inside the Torino penalty area. The Georgian converted from the penalty spot to give his side a slightly unwarranted two-goal lead going into half-time. The wind was knocked from the sails of Ivan Juriç's side and Napoli pounced. Osimhen doubled his tally after the break, and Tanguy Ndombélé swept home a fourth after Napoli pressed and won possession high in Torino's half. Spalletti's side had passed a tough assignment and won convincingly without playing anywhere near their best. Many consider results like these to be the hallmark of champions.

Speaking of champions, Napoli would face reigning Serie A title-holders Milan three times in the next two weeks. The first was at home in Serie A before the highly anticipated Champions League quarter-finals in mid-April. Napoli were dealt a major blow in the days before the first of the trilogy when Osimhen was ruled out with a muscle injury. Giovanni Simeone and Giacomo Raspadori had stepped in superbly in the autumn when Osimhen had missed over four weeks with a similar injury, but since his return Napoli's number nine had hit new scoring levels. Deputising for one of Europe's form players was a huge ask, and Spalletti turned to Simeone to do so from the start.

On the other bench, Stefano Pioli fielded his preferred 4-2-3-1 but deployed Ismaël Bennacer in the more advanced position rather than as part of the double pivot. The Algerian is a high-quality operator from deep, both as a distributor but also in his defensive work. His inclusion in a higher starting position was a clear tactical statement from Pioli: Bennacer would be used to suffocate Stanislav Lobotka at the base of Napoli's midfield and allow the other two Milan midfielders to tend to André-Frank Zambo Anguissa and Piotr Zieliński. Milan had won the title a year previous on the foundations provided by an industrious midfield that won the ball and moved it quickly, if not expansively. This was a clear return to that philosophy.

Milan wasted no time in hitting Napoli on their own turf. Rafael Leão darted between centre-backs Kim Min-jae and Amir Rrahmani before delightfully dinking over Alex Meret. The Portuguese winger had won last season's Most Valuable Player award for 11 goals and 10 assists in Milan's title-winning side. His electric pace, trickery and Thierry Henry-esque capacity to open his body up to finish into the far corner had marked Leão out as one of the league's best players. The rise of 'Kvaradona' had ignited conversations about who was better, with the Georgian enjoying a more impactful season than the Milan winger. Leão's performance at the Maradona added further fuel to the debate. He was involved again eight minutes later, drifting centrally to link play before Brahim Diaz lashed in Milan's second. Napoli were being picked off on the counter-attack and were unable to lay a glove on Leão. Milan's third was scored in an almost identical fashion: their gritty midfield pinched the ball and in one pass cut through Napoli's retreating defence. Leão made Amir Rrahmani dance as he twisted right and left, and put Napoli out of their misery with a brutal left-footed shot. A shell-shocked Stadio Diego Armando Maradona somehow grew quieter still when Alexis Saelemakers eased through a series of limp challenges to then slide in Milan's fourth.

Napoli had been schooled by the champions in what was their second home defeat in three in the league. They had missed the outlet Osimhen provided with his runs into wide channels, hunting down lost causes and offering a long-ball threat when needed. The most telling indication of the job performed on Napoli was Lobotka being substituted in the 67th minute. The match had already gone with Milan 4-0 up, but Lobotka was the lynchpin of Napoli's work. Everything went through him, so Milan sought to disrupt him at every turn. It worked. Spalletti was distraught, but not by what he saw on the pitch. Weeks later, after the first Champions League tie against the same opposition,

Spalletti described the atmosphere at the Maradona during the 4-0 defeat as 'absurd'. 'If the same thing happens in the return match, I'll leave the bench and go home. It's an inexplicable thing. The boys are sensitive to what happens around them and against Milan at the Maradona we played in an absurd atmosphere. We were taken hostage.' (*Goal*)

Amid all the euphoria and celebratory spirit curated during that season, Napoli's fanbase was at war with itself and the club owner during the loss to Milan. Club president Aurelio De Laurentiis had announced plans to increase ticket prices, and the club ultras responded with a silent protest during the match. Conceding four goals to a rival would silence any supporter group, but this was an altogether different proposition. Napoli's display did little to lift the muted fans, but those fans also began brawling and fighting in the stadium as the match wore on. This is the 'absurd' atmosphere to which Spalletti referred. *La Repubblica* (via *Football Italia*) stated that the protesting ultras were the same group that had demonstrated during Spalletti's and De Laurentiis' pre-season appearance about the club's transfer business. The furore surrounding ticketing was the most publicised reason for the protests, but grievances also included issues of stricter security measures in the stadium, a proposed membership ticket system, and bans on banners and flags. In short, the protests were not united against one common theme but rather against everything De Laurentiis had proposed. It is unsurprising that a flashpoint was created amongst such passionate (if uncoordinated) demonstrations.

Whilst the nine months that followed proved the squad overhaul to be a masterstroke from De Laurentiis and sporting director Cristiano Giuntoli, there remained a fury and discontent towards the club owner. *Football Italia* reported that there were chants before the match declaring De Laurentiis to be 'the proprietor and not the master of the club'. This magnificent campaign had turned any ill feeling towards Luciano Spalletti into pure adoration. The same could not be said for De Laurentiis, who was even assigned police protection in the weeks that followed the protests.

From a purely statistical perspective, the defeat cut Napoli's 19-point advantage to 16 as Lazio beat Monza 2-0 to reinforce their claim for second place. The dream scenario of winning the title away to Juventus now looked unlikely, and matchweek 32 was pencilled in as the new possible coronation date: on Saturday, 30 March 2023, at home to Salernitana.

Napoli bounced back from the Milan horror show by beating Lecce 2-1, but again the performance was a far cry from their exhilarating best. Napoli may have begun to stutter, but Giovanni Di Lorenzo was taking his performances to a new level. Captains can develop an intuition for when to elevate their own game, especially when those around them are tiring. The Italian had not only led by example all season, but established himself as one of Europe's best right-backs. Di Lorenzo opened the scoring on the Ionian coast, but it took an own goal from Antonio Gallo to beat the side in 16th place.

An enormous 68% possession and 656 passes kept Napoli in control of the ball, but they mustered just nine shots from such dominance. For context, Lecce attempted two more. Giovanni Simeone was swapped out for Giacomo Raspadori and the diminutive Italian failed to make an impression, touching the ball just 26 times and attempting one shot in his 65 minutes. Even Kvaratskhelia looked bereft of ideas. With Osimhen still unavailable, opposition defences were no longer stretched trying to contain the pair and could now focus their efforts on locking down the Georgian.

Nevertheless, three points were taken back to Naples, a welcome release of pressure before the second instalment of the Napoli–Milan trilogy. The first leg of the Champions League quarter-final took place at San Siro, where Napoli had beaten Milan 2-1 in September but lost 1-0 to Inter straight after the World Cup break. Unsurprisingly, *I Rossoneri* were unchanged from the pair's recent encounter. Spalletti on the other hand played an altogether different hand to anything he had throughout the season. Both Simeone and Raspadori had flattered to deceive in the two matches Osimhen had missed, so Spalletti changed tack by playing without a recognised striker. Eljif Elmas had already covered central midfield and both wing positions in 2022/23, and the North Macedonian was now to play as a false nine. The idea was to free up Matteo Politano and Kvaratskhelia on the wings, whilst also allowing Napoli to overrun the midfield when Elmas dropped deep to create a numerical advantage. The logic was sound, and Elmas had proven himself to be intelligent and skilled enough to carry it out.

As the players lined up under the hallowed chimes of the Champions League music, one long side of San Siro spelled out 'THIS IS MILAN' in white. One short side, the Curva Sud where Milan's ultras are situated, unfurled a spectacular *tifo*. Two enormous red hands hovered above a small, cowering figure as if they were to strangle it. The figure was that of 'Pulcinella', a masked puppet who had become an icon of Naples. A cunning and devious character, Pulcinella embodied the impish spirit of the Neapolitan. It is reported that Luciano Spalletti even presented each visiting coach with their own Pulcinella miniature throughout the season. It was a magnificent display of fan choreography, and foreshadowed an evening of high intensity and fabled rivalry.

Two of Italy's most respected and seasoned tacticians were about to battle it out again. Within 60 seconds Napoli nearly had the lead. Kvaratskhelia received the ball on the left side of the penalty area and had a simple side-foot finish cleared off the line by Davide Calabria. It was the response Napoli needed to eradicate the demons of the 4-0 at the Maradona, but Kvaratskhelia could not provide the finishing touch. Zambo Anguissa and Kvaratskhelia had sights of goal in the following ten minutes, and Zieliński forced a leaping save from goalkeeper Mike Maignan from range. One of the notable impacts of Victor Osimhen's absence had been that Napoli's midfield were having to carry more of the scoring burden without having their strengths played to by the Nigerian's link play and defender-pulling gravity. The result was that Napoli were shooting from range more as the wingers and full-backs worked the ball back to the edge of the penalty area, and not towards the six-yard box where Osimhen would so often lurk. Napoli were testing Maignan's goal without truly feeling like they were clicking into gear.

Their chief tormentor a week prior had been Rafael Leão and the Portuguese nearly added to his brace that night, only to slide his finish past the far post. Amir Rrahmani would have lost sleep after what Leão had done to him at the Maradona, and the sight of the Portuguese running at him again would have sent shivers down the Kosovan's spine. As it had been in Naples, Milan found the Napoli gameplan falling right into their hands. Napoli would hold the ball for long periods of time, teasing and probing at Milan before eventually losing possession in the final third. Milan invited Napoli's aggressive press deep in their half and played through it with a quick exchange before releasing the jet-heeled Leão. Time and time again Napoli were suckered in and bypassed to leave Giovanni Di Lorenzo in a foot race with Leão. No right-back in world football wins that race. Unsurprisingly, the opening goal came in transition. Leão went right, Brahim Diaz and Ismaël Bennacer went left and the Algerian blasted into the roof of Alex Meret's net.

Where Milan's goals in Naples had been met by eerie silence, Bennacer's strike ignited an explosion of noise in the wet Milanese night. Napoli created the occasional opening, but their task was made all the harder when Zambo Anguissa was shown two yellow cards in four second-half minutes to reduce them to ten men. Milan had Napoli's number, and had beaten them again. The 1-0 scoreline may have looked kinder than the previous defeat at Milan's hands, but the reality remained the same. Napoli's main attacking threat was captain Di Lorenzo from right-back, taking five shots. The combination of Milan's tailored tactics and the Osimhen-shaped hole was hurting Napoli just as their season was supposed to be hitting its crescendo.

Osimhen made his long-awaited return at home to Hellas Verona in the league match that followed, named among the substitutes. Spalletti turned to Serie A's top scorer just after the hour mark with the scores locked at 0-0 and Raspadori continuing to struggle as the attacking focal point. The coach had made significant changes to his side in an attempt to rest and rejuvenate those that had played nearly every available match in the season. Rare starts were handed to the lesser-spotted Diego Demme in midfield and Juan Jesus at the heart of defence, and even Kvaratskhelia was rested. Such changes did little to restore fluency and Napoli once again struggled to create as their patient build-up became laboured and stunted. The return of Osimhen alone would not fix these issues. A 0-0 draw against 18th-placed Hellas was a disappointing return and meant that Napoli had taken only ten points from their last 18 available – far from disastrous, but a world away from the side that had dropped just seven points from the first 24 rounds combined. Spalletti's frustrations were becoming evident. 'We had less quality than ever, we created some space but we were not good at playing in that space,' bemoaned the Tuscan afterwards (*Reuters*). Spalletti even went as far as to celebrate Osimhen's return by comparing his quality to those around him: 'In the last 25 minutes he has shown that he has greater potential than the others.'

Spalletti and the club were pronounced in their efforts to cool expectation of Osimhen's return, stating his need to be integrated slowly following the injury. However, there was no doubting that Osimhen would be available to start the second leg against Milan at the Maradona. They trailed by one goal on aggregate, and the opportunity to send Napoli to their first Champions League semi-final was the kind of occasion that Osimhen lives for. The teamsheets arrived for the second leg with Napoli's number nine restored to the side as the most notable change. For the final part of this enthralling, Milan-dominated saga, Pioli's side were unchanged again.

After all the trauma inflicted in the two recent defeats, a victory here would be Napoli's redemption. The 4-0 battering could be reframed in hindsight as a tired champion-elect missing a step, and the first-leg defeat as a wake-up call before the main event. The two defeats without scoring would have an asterisk next to them, with Napoli's progression to the final four of the Champions League taking over the narrative. With the league title now all but confirmed (even if they were limping over the line), the story could take an altogether more spectacular turn if they could become champions of Europe too. At 1-0 down and playing the second leg at home with Osimhen returning, the dream was on.

Napoli began with the bit between their teeth. Gone was the Maradona's sweeping silence, replaced by a ferocious and expectant intensity. In the first 20 minutes, Napoli attempted seven shots before Milan could muster their first. Kvaratskhelia was rejuvenated by Osimhen's presence and afforded the space to impart his influence. Then in the 21st minute, the tie took a familiar turn. Milan broke forward having been camped inside their own half for the match's duration. Rafael Leão laid the ball off for

Brahim Diaz, and a late challenge from Mário Rui wiped him out. Penalty given.

Many inside the Maradona closed their eyes, head bowed, waiting for the rustle of ball in net and the distant cheer of travelling Milanisti. Instead, they heard the whump of ball slamming into Alex Meret's gloves. Penalty saved, and crisis averted. Giroud followed up his miss by forcing another save from Meret minutes later. The chance arose from Juan Jesus' tentative pass out from the back, having first rolled an unconvincing ball back to his goalkeeper. The Brazilian had replaced Kim Min-jae at centre-back with the South Korean suspended, slotting in on the left side as a left-footed centre-back. Such adjustments may seem small, but the change in angle can alter a team's chemistry and the way they shift the ball around after a whole season of having the right-footed Kim playing there.

Over the last two weeks Napoli had been served numerous reminders of Rafael Leão's quality. When Giovanni Di Lorenzo closes his eyes at night, he will likely still see the tall winger bearing down on him to this day. His two goals at the Maradona were breathtaking, but Leão was about to serve up something just as special. Collecting the ball inside his own half, Leão started off at a canter. His long and easy stride eats up the turf so effortlessly that it can be hard to gauge how fast he is moving. Di Lorenzo stepped up and stuck a leg out to halt him, which Leão bypassed with ease. Rrahmani lunged in next and Leão stepped over his attempts. The final bit was easy, as Leão rolled the ball across for Giroud to finish into a nearly empty net. Leão's mockery knew no bounds as he continued to do the unthinkable at Napoli's expense.

Napoli were now 2-0 down on aggregate. Osimhen had been starved of service, and his most telling contribution was a low finish that beat Mike Maignan only for the referee to correctly disallow it for a handball. After half-time, his partner in crime Kvaratskhelia rolled the clock back to late 2022 with a dazzling piece of skill to beat Davide Calabria on the byline and thump a shot past Maignan's far post. Had it been late 2022, the ball would probably have rocketed into the net, and not out for a goal kick.

The Georgian continued to grow into the match, and had his chance to equalise when Napoli were awarded a penalty for a handball in the 82nd minute. With Leão having taken the tie by the throat, this was Kvaratskhelia's opportunity to respond. However, not for the first time in the season, the penalty would not be converted. Kvaratskhelia sent Maignan diving to his right and the Frenchman saved brilliantly. The Maradona's silence had returned, but Napoli kept going. In the depth of added time, Osimhen had his moment. Amongst a crowded penalty area, Osimhen found an inch of room to power a header into the bottom corner to level the scores in the 93rd minute.

It was to be the final act of a thrilling encounter, as Milan celebrated wildly. Over the two legs, Pioli's side had managed Napoli perfectly and were worthy progressors. For the first time in the season, Napoli were heartbroken. Each to a man collapsed on the Maradona's turf as the dream of a first Champions League semi-final disappeared. Having congratulated Milan, Spalletti emphasised his pride in his players. 'I also want to congratulate my players. We played a Champions League campaign of the highest level and we played a good match tonight. We paid for a little inexperience in reading the moments of the match.'

The club president was less magnanimous than his coach. Weeks later, De Laurentiis said that Napoli had been 'the strongest team' in the Champions League and that 'just because the referee was not good twice, we are out. That is soccer, that is UEFA, that is the world.'

There had been a sense that Napoli's magical domestic season would carry them to European glory too. Their displays in the group stages had won fans across Europe and kick-started the euphoria that carried them to their enormous lead in the Serie A table. Whilst a quarter-final finish might not immediately seem like a catalyst for one of the club's greatest ever campaigns, its role in generating momentum for Spalletti's juggernaut cannot be overstated. Some of the most striking memories of Napoli's glorious 2022/23 season were created not in Serie A, but on the European stage. It will forever be a part of the season's story. Devastation sat heavily on the face of Napoli's players that night, but it was reported that the Maradona echoed with victory song. Fans sang of their hearts being full of hope as they sat on the precipice of delivering that treasured third Scudetto.

* * *

Eight matches remained of the 2022/23 season. Napoli's lead sat at 14 points, with Lazio on 61 points in second place. With any realistic debate about the title gone by February, the more finely poised narrative was that of the chase for Champions League spots. Lazio had a five-point advantage on third-place Milan, but the 2021/22 champions, Roma, Inter, Atalanta and Juventus were separated by just seven points. Napoli still had fixtures to play against Juventus, Inter, and a highly impressive Bologna side aiming for Europe themselves. Their recent stuttering form had evaporated conversations of where they would like to win the title, and had become a matter of getting it sealed as quickly as possible and hoping results fell their way.

In matchweek 31, Napoli had their first stroke of luck in what felt like weeks as Lazio lost at home to Torino. Should Napoli win late on Sunday night, the title could feasibly be won the following weekend at home to Salernitana if Lazio failed to beat Inter. In Sunday's late kick-off, regarded as the prime spot for Serie A's biggest fixtures of the weekend, Napoli travelled to Juventus. They had had a five-day break since the Champions League heartbreak, and Spalletti refused to speak to the press in the build-up to the match. Whether this was an attempt to close ranks and reduce the noise surrounding the fixture's magnitude is uncertain. The coach had used his press conferences to highlight the shift in atmosphere that had accompanied their recent dip in form, and the protests that had marred the fixtures with Milan. Juventus veersus Napoli rarely needs amplifying. It is a storied match, with a history of infamous incidents, title-deciding moments and deep-rooted bad blood. Spalletti's silence furthered the impression that this iteration was going to add to the lore.

Napoli tweaked their line-up from the side that had played Milan in Naples earlier in the week. Piotr Zieliński was rested as Tanguy Ndombélé started alongside Zambo Anguissa in the more advanced midfield roles. Hirving Lozano and Matteo Politano performed their now-ritualistic switching, with the Mexican replacing the Italian on the right flank. Mário Rui was absent from the squad altogether and was deputised for by Mathías Oliveira. Juventus benched their two leading attacking stars in Dusan Vlahovic and Federico Chiesa, with neither recapturing their best form. This was a new-look side, dotted with academy talents like Fabio Miretti and Mathías Soulé, but hunkered down into Allegri's 4-4-1-1. Lessons had been learned from the 5-1 battering taken at the Maradona, and Allegri was out to stifle the league leaders as they placed one hand on the Scudetto.

Napoli laboured through the first half, short of inspiration and restricted by Juventus' low block. That 4-4-1-1 collapsed into a low-lying 4-5-1 when the visitors had possession, and sought to block the route from the Napoli midfield into Osimhen and Kvaratskhelia. Ndombélé sought to influence proceedings in a rare start, and was lively in his attempts. Like Zambo Anguissa, the Frenchman thrives in collecting the ball from his defence and driving forward. In full flight, Ndombélé is a delight to watch. His game is littered with drops of the shoulder to shimmy away from pressure, snappy passes delivered through the lines without a backlift, and lolloping strides across the ground. He was taken off just after an hour, but the midfielder was fouled three times and completed five progressive carries; only Kvaratskhelia (seven) and Lozano (six) completed more in the match. Napoli camped in the

Juventus half, shifting the ball from side to side without being able to find their forward line.

The home side sat, waited and crunched every heavy touch or miscontrolled pass. Osimhen fed on scraps but sought to shoot on sight, as is his trademark. Six shots in the match only found the target twice, but Osimhen could have scored three in the space of five second-half minutes. The first skimmed off the near post with Wojciech Szczęsny motionless. Then Osimhen headed from a corner straight at the Juventus goalkeeper. His leap was every bit as impressive as the one he had scored with in the reverse fixture, but this time the finish was tame. The third was archetypal Napoli under Spalletti. Giovanni Di Lorenzo spotted Osimhen's run and carved a pass over the Juventus defence and into the penalty area's right side. Osimhen raced on to it and lashed a rising shot over the crossbar. Napoli had found the chink in Juventus' armour as they played quicker and more directly. Still the goal wouldn't come, however.

Then came the twist. Juventus flew up the other end in transition, and Ángel Di María fired past Alex Meret via a deflection. Even at their lowest ebb in a punishing season (in every sense), Juventus had found a way to wound Napoli again. As the Allianz Arena erupted, referee Michael Fabbri was summoned to the pitchside monitor to review a potential foul in the build-up from Arkadiusz Milik on Stanislav Lobotka. The contact was minimal, but Fabbri deemed it strong enough to reverse the decision, and the goal was disallowed. Aurelio Di Laurentiis might be quick to lament referees when decision go against Napoli, but here a referee's call had saved them. Six minutes of regular time, plus any added on. Napoli had been spared, but still had to find a goal themselves. Incredibly, Juventus thought they had scored again when Vlahoviç came off the bench and found the net in stoppage time. This too was ruled out when a replay showed the ball to have gone out of play prior to Federico Chiesa's cross. After two reprieves and multiple squandered opportunities, Napoli had to make it count.

Spalletti turned to his bench and brought on Giacomo Raspadori to replace Kvaratskhelia. 'Kvaradona' had struggled throughout the match, and had embarked on a barren run of form in going five matches across all competitions without a goal contribution. The longest spell he had experienced without a goal or assist before had been just three league matches. Osimhen's absence had hurt him greatly as opposition defences could now double and even triple up on him, safe in the knowledge that the Nigerian did not require their attention. Kvaratskhelia was far from his devastating best but removing him for 'Jack' Raspadori, who himself had not scored since October, raised eyebrows.

With 93 of the 96 minutes played, Napoli came forward down the right. Substitutes Piotr Zieliński and Eljif Elmas combined with far greater space than any Napoli player had experienced throughout the match. Elmas' cross was surely destined for Osimhen, stood up and flighted for the striker to launch himself at. It flew over Osimhen's head and towards Raspadori, eight yards from goal and left of centre. Raspadori's eyes never fell from the ball's path, and he swung his left foot through it on the volley. Goal. 1-0 Napoli. Like so many of the great and iconic goals, the celebration to watch wasn't of the scorer himself, but of those around him. As Raspadori tore away, eyes widened and mouth agape, Zieliński collapsed on the other side of the pitch, spreadeagled upon his back.

'Raspadori's goal against Juventus in Turin last April wasn't *the* goal that clinched the Scudetto, but it made it feel an inevitability,' wrote James Horncastle for *The Athletic*. Napoli fans had dreamt of winning the title in Turin, and whilst their patchy form had denied this possibility, victory that night had all but confirmed their crowning. Should Lazio fail to beat Inter at San Siro on Saturday, Napoli would be crowned Serie A champions with a win against Salernitana in Naples. As the Napoli bus made its way back into the city in the early hours of the morning, swarms of fans awaited them, almost lifting the team back to their headquarters. The title was not confirmed, but Neapolitans now knew that they could be there to see it won at home on Saturday, 30 April 2023.

The weeks building up to the final weekend of April had been rife with speculation about when the title would be won. As it emerged that Salernitana's visit would be the most likely fixture for Napoli to mathematically seal the Scudetto, Ben Bocsak bought a flight and a match ticket. This was no longer just an event for Naples to celebrate; to be present when Napoli became champions of Italy after 30 years of hurt was a footballing pilgrimage that had to be taken. Ben was one of the lucky tourists to be there. 'As soon as I left the airport every street was surrounded by blue and white ribbons. It was as if it were a carnival, and a kind of football fever like no other with days still to go before the match,' he tells me. 'Football here matters more.'

Ben is a football writer of the highest standard. We have worked together on projects for the best part of four years, and remain good friends. His videos and photos kept me glued to my phone that weekend as I tried to live vicariously through him. The days before the match saw him experience the Spanish quarter. 'Everyone went to the Maradona mural on the day before the match, singing and dancing. I have never seen anything like it. The atmosphere was so special, and you could tell that the locals were living and breathing Napoli.'

The meeting with Salernitana had been scheduled to happen on the Saturday, but it was postponed by a day along with Lazio's visit to Inter. Napoli fans would be glued to their screens to see if Inter could deliver them their moment by taking points off Maurizio Sarri's team in the early Sunday kick-off. Celebratory as the atmosphere was, Luciano Spalletti had to maintain composure amidst the euphoria. 'I don't like to celebrate in advance. If we all do it together, there will be twice as much joy.' (*The Athletic*). Spalletti had boycotted his press duties before the victory in Turin, but here he was at his flowing, expressive best.

Spalletti said: 'If you love someone or something, the only thing you can dedicate to them is time. That shows how much you love them, and I have dedicated it all to them [the team].' Spalletti went on to describe his emotions ahead of the match: 'I get excited easily. I'm scared if I think back to where I started. I already had the emotion when I passed the stadium on the roadside, and tomorrow more.' Spalletti also discussed the importance of waiting. 'This waiting and the difficulty of being unfulfilled [sic] have been worth it. Experiencing this with Napoli, I am glad it has been so. It's the stuff you have to wait a few more games for.'

That sense of waiting could mean many things. Waiting to be crowned champions having established a formidable lead months ago, and the club's three-decade wait for a title. It also speaks of his own patience and waiting. Having come so close with Roma and being nearly chased out of Naples a season before, Spalletti's patience had been every bit as impressive as Napoli's. In January, Spalletti had overtaken Carlo Ancelotti as the manager with the most Serie A wins in the three-points-for-a-win era, with his 276th victory. By the end of the season, only Carlo Mazzone (797), Nereo Rocco (748), Giovanni Trapattoni (689) and Nils Liedholm (644) could better Spalletti's 559 matches in charge, and only the latter three had taken more than his 996 points across those matches. This was his title, as well as Napoli's.

'Outside the stadium there were flares going off every second,' recalls Ben. 'We went through the turnstiles two hours early and were listening to Inter vs Lazio, as everything depended on that game.' Inter beat Lazio 3-1, putting Simone Inzaghi's side back in the top three after a rocky season. It also meant that three points against Salernitana that same day would crown Napoli. 'When we heard the result had gone Napoli's way, the noise inside the half-filled Maradona was as if Mount Vesuvius had erupted. People were in tears, hugging and looking up at the sky.' Naples had decided: today they would be champions.

Napoli were welcomed on to the pitch to a cacophonous roar. The 11 players that day were almost identical to the 11 shirts that hung in formation in the Spanish quarter, with the only exception being Mathías Oliveira's continued stay at left-back. Osimhen spearheaded Napoli's early attacks, flashing a header wide and then directing one straight at the goalkeeper as crosses poured in. With each chance that came, the noise lifted and then sank in a disheartened 'ahhh' in between honking horns and drum beats. The first half produced ten shots, of which nine came from Napoli, as Salernitana rarely threatened to foray forward. Kvaratskhelia was involved in three shot-creating actions in the first 45 minutes alone as he enjoyed the freedom created by Osimhen's presence.

Just after an hour of action, Spalletti rolled the changes and introduced the hero of Turin, Giacomo Raspadori. Within two minutes of his introduction, Raspadori created another iconic moment. His outswinging cross bent out to the edge of the six-yard box to be headed in by Oliveira. Pandemonium ensued. The Uruguayan had scored just one goal prior, in a 4-1 win over Cremonese back in October, and duly hurdled the advertising hoardings with captain Giovanni Di Lorenzo to drink in the celebrations. The camera shook under the weight of Naples' outpouring and smoke lifted from outside the Stadio Diego Armando Maradona. The celebrations were so wild that the tremor was recorded at 2.0 on the Richter scale (*Corriere Dello Sport*). Napoli's title charge had officially reached earth-shattering proportions, without the need for a metaphor. Fuorigrotta was shaking.

The lead was nearly doubled, and the title sealed, with ten minutes remaining. Kvaratskhelia slipped a swinging left-footed shot past the far post, with a frustrated Victor

Osimhen alone in the penalty area. Salernitana dared to creep forward having produced a mere three shots in the match. And then it came. Boulaye Dia cut in from the right, with no Napoli player making the challenge to bring him down. Dia whipped a shot into the far corner, and the Maradona swallowed itself in silence. A quiet grief born out of delirium. 'I have never heard silence like it,' remembers Ben. 'It felt like someone had come to break up a party. I walked back home for an hour from the stadium and everyone was a little sullen. When I ate at a restaurant later, there were still many Napoli shirts but they were a little bit down. Their eyes didn't glimmer like they did the day before. Later that night it started to rain – and then it rained the next day as well. It felt like a real downer after all the excitement.'

Spalletti smiled and poured positivity over the anti-climax of the draw. 'As far as I am concerned, this just extends the enjoyment. It just carries on the celebration a little longer, as I am convinced we'll get those points.' Those points were in fact just one required point. A draw away to Udinese would give Napoli an unassailable 16-point lead with five matches remaining.

A midweek evening in Udine was not how Napoli had pictured winning the Scudetto. The weekend's draw with Salernitana had felt like the boiling point of emotion, and the perfect moment for all of the frustration and delight to spill out in equal measure. Udinese's Stadio Friuli is the best part of nine hours away from the Maradona by car, and is a tricky stadium to access. With it being so difficult to travel to the Italian-Croatian border on a Thursday night, Stadio Diego Armando Maradona was turned into a makeshift cinema for fans to watch the match. Over 50,000 fans attended, with a fraction of that able to be in attendance in Udine. It had been rumoured that Napoli fans had infiltrated the home sections and wore black, waiting for the moment where they could celebrate as their true selves.

They were made to wait. Udinese took the lead as Napoli continued to stumble towards the finish line. Despite being in need of an equalising goal, *I Partenopei* attempted just seven shots all match. The 0.5xG they mustered across the 90 minutes was their joint-lowest of the season. However, all they needed was a goal, and Victor Osimhen stood up amidst the tired and fatiguing blue shirts. The Nigerian stuck a finish into the top corner after a series of rebounds and blocks, and from there in it was a case of preserving their lead. The irony could not be lost that Napoli, who had illuminated the continent with a campaign of glorious attacking football, were about to claim their treasured league title on the back of a wretched performance 850km away.

One win in seven had wearied the same players that had driven Napoli to their best-ever start to a Serie A season. It mattered not, however. The final whistle blew, and pandemonium in Udine ensued. Fans streamed on to the pitch and began digging it up for their own slice of history. Spalletti and his players were mobbed and paraded as idols. Piotr Zieliński could be spotted in the crowd as he had stripped to his underwear. Back in Naples, fireworks filled the sky and the honking of horns dotted the evening air. This emotional city in an emotional country sobbed and roared, and laughed and rejoiced. Both in Fuorigrotta and Udine, Diego Maradona's face swung high above the masses. In their darkest and brightest times, Maradona's presence is always keenly felt. It was not all a case of celebration, as a 26-year-old Napoli fan was shot after an altercation with Udinese ultras. Even on the pitch in Udine there were violent clashes between the supporters as Udinese fans required police intervention while the players were still on the pitch.

Napoli had broken the north's chokehold on Italian football. Roma in 2000/01 were the last non-northern side to win Serie A as Milan, Inter and Juventus between them collected the 20 titles that followed. Luciano Spalletti had also become the oldest coach to win it, at 64 years old. 'Seeing Neapolitans happy is enough to give you a sense of that joy they are feeling,' said Spalletti. 'These people will look to this moment when life gets hard, they have every right to celebrate like this.'

'I'm happy for all Neapolitans worldwide,' remarked Osimhen. 'No one deserves the Scudetto more than Neapolitans, more than us. I want to enjoy this moment for the rest of my life!' An emotional Giovanni Di Lorenzo was the first captain since Diego Maradona to win a league title with Napoli. 'Being compared to him, being the captain after Maradona to lift the Scudetto, I just have no words. It is not my Scudetto, it belongs to all the players and all the people who worked to make this dream come true.'

Aurelio De Laurentiis was at the Maradona with the Napoli fans to see the title won. 'When I arrived in Naples, I said in the first ten years, I will bring you in Europe and I made [good on that promise] earlier than ten years. And I said also in the second ten years we will win the Scudetto and also that time was two years earlier. Now we have begun a new era and we hope to win next year and the following year and the following year.' The president continued: 'You always told me, we want to win. And we won! We all won together. And on Sunday against Fiorentina, everyone here for the big party. Thank you to everyone!'

Napoli's recent form was the least important matter to consider, but the inconsistencies continued even after the official crowning. The following home match against Fiorentina began with a guard of honour as the visiting players acknowledged the league champions, but *I Partenopei* still lacked the spark of previous months. Victor Osimhen scored a penalty (having missed one earlier in the match) as Spalletti's side squeezed to a 1-0 victory. They were then beaten 2-0 away to Monza and then, seemingly from nowhere, rallied impressively in the second half to score three times in a home win over Inter (albeit Inter were down to ten men for over 50 minutes).

The mood, both at home and on the road, naturally remained euphoric. Banners flew, smoke flares billowed blue through the air, and each and every player glowed. During this run, Osimhen's pursuit of the top scorer mantle was relentless. Against Bologna he scored twice from five shots in just 65 minutes of action. The second was the perfect example of how far Osimhen's game had come. A crowded Bologna penalty area was broken apart as Osimhen let a simple pass into this feet roll past him, taking two defenders out of the game. The finish shot along the turf into the far corner for the Nigerian's 25th Serie A goal of the season. He was now four clear of Lautaro

Martínez and would almost certainly finish the season as the *capocannoniere*, becoming the first African player to do so. Goal number 26 followed in the season's closing fixture at home to Sampdoria, and Osimhen became the first player to win both the *capocannoniere* and Scudetto in the same season since Zlatan Ibrahimović in 2008/09.

It is undeniable that his best patch had been in the early stage of 2023 as he scored in eight consecutive Serie A matches. However, after Napoli stumbled in his spring absence, his return almost single-handedly dragged them over the line. It was Osimhen that scored in Udine, and seven league goals from the start of March essentially guaranteed his status as Serie A's best striker that season. By comparison, Khvicha Kvaratskhelia endured a barren spell of just one assist and no goals in the final 11 matches of the season.

Wind forward six months, and Osimhen was crowned AIC (Italian Footballers' Association) Player of the Year for 2022/23, as well as featuring in the AIC Serie A Team of the Year alongside team-mates Giovanni Di Lorenzo, Kim Min-jae, Stanislav Lobotka and Khvicha Kvaratskhelia. Osimhen added to his collection of titles and silverware by being named 2023 African Player of the Year, and finished eighth in the Ballon d'Or 2023 votes for the world's best player.

Back to Naples, and the final match of Napoli's winning season. Osimhen's penalty put Napoli ahead, and Giovanni Simeone scored with an audacious effort from outside of the penalty area. It was a fittingly wonderful whipped effort, celebrated by a blue-haired Simeone holding the shirt of Maradona aloft, a 77th and final goal of the season that took Napoli to 90 points, and closed 2022/23. The Maradona had been fitted with temporary concert screens prior to kick-off that allowed every spectator a closer look as Giovanni Di Lorenzo hoisted the trophy aloft. For the first time since Diego Maradona inspired Napoli to the 1989/90 Scudetto, Napoli were champions of Italy.

Unsurprisingly, Luciano Spalletti was named Coach of the Year. Despite his poor run of form towards the end of the season, Khvicha Kvaratskhelia was crowned Most Valuable Player for his 12 goals and 13 assists (plus two goals and four assists in the Champions League) in his first season in a top-five league: a remarkable ascent to stardom for an unknown player signed in the midst of severe fan dissatisfaction and turmoil.

Nothing could tarnish the joy and history-making success of 2022/23. Its mark was left on the city and on its coach, who revealed a tattoo on his forearm of the Napoli crest above the Scudetto shield as the trophy was paraded across the Maradona's turf. However, in a manner that suits Napoli's character and personality almost too perfectly, the narrative would soon take an unexpected and remarkable turn.

Who were Luciano Spalletti's Napoli?

THREE MORE goals scored, four fewer conceded, and 11 more points than the previous season. Napoli's leap from third-placed nearly-men to champions appears to be a case study in fine tuning an already functioning machine. Luciano Spalletti said himself that the realistic target was not to win the title, but consolidate their footing in the Champions League after an impressive 2021/22 season. The nature of their tail-off in Spalletti's first season had created a false impression of a title-ready side that collapsed at the critical moment. Their electric first half-season had raised the bar, and Napoli fans could once again dream of ending their three-decade curse. If anything, their decline as Inter and Milan pulled clear reinforced Spalletti's belief that his team was not ready to compete at the very top of the league over a 38-match season. The marginal gains that increased their points tally by 11 points and improved their goal difference cannot alone explain how Napoli went on to win the 2022/23 Scudetto.

Before diving into the tactical and systemic elements of this team, the contending elements and factors outside of Napoli's control must first be discussed. Front and centre of this debate is the deterioration of their rivals. The previous season's champions, Milan, returned 16 fewer points in their 2022/23 title defence. Inter, runners-up to their city rivals a year before, finished the next season with 72 points, 12 less than their second-place finish. Then there were Juventus, who after having points stripped, then returned, and then taken away again, were eight points worse off than their 70-point return in 2021/22. Of the top six (excluding Napoli), Lazio and Atalanta were the only clubs to improve or finish higher in the league table.

Juventus' situation has already been discussed, but the demise of the Milan clubs undoubtedly smoothed Napoli's ascent. *I Rossoneri* were comfortably Napoli's toughest opponent across the season, beating Spalletti's side twice in four Serie A and Champions League meetings. On a tactical level, Milan were a team well-suited to negating Napoli's threat. Even at their Scudetto-winning best, Milan's best work came off the ball with an aggressive midfield press that turned the ball over and fed their attackers and high-flying full-backs quickly. Theirs was a side built on functionality in the middle of the pitch above individual quality, and a mindset without ego or preconceptions of dominating the ball. In 2021/22 the blueprint was fairly simple: strip the ball off the opponent and give it to one of Theo Hernández or Rafael Leão. It was this exact model that tore apart Napoli at the Maradona in early April in a ruthless display of fast counter-attacking. Napoli's high defensive line left them exposed, and Milan's pacy attack wreaked havoc. Their performances against Napoli were the high point in an underwhelming season. As brilliant as Hernández and Leão are, their threat from the left tilted Milan overwhelmingly towards them. On the opposite side of the pitch Milan's options were far less threatening, and allowed opponents to negate their threat by stacking defenders and man-marking midfielders around the left-sided duo.

Then there was Inter. They and Milan had pulled clear of Napoli and were delivering a sensational city-based title race. Then came an away trip to Bologna in April 2022, when second-choice goalkeeper Ionut Radu was dispossessed yards from his goal line to allow Bologna to score and win. That was seen as the defining moment of the title race and swung momentum back in Milan's favour. It also marked the end of Radu's time in Milan, or at least for the foreseeable future as the Romanian was sent out on loan for the next two seasons. Head coach Simone Inzaghi was under enormous strain and ultimately kept his job by winning the Coppa Italia and making the UEFA Champions League Final. The momentum gathered off the back of such a run carried into the next season, when Inter would win the Scudetto with a team that could be deemed every bit as strong and potent as Napoli's of 2022/23.

That season had shown that Inter under Inzaghi continued to be a phenomenal cup team, and the one that followed stated their claim as one of the great modern Serie A sides. However, it also proved that Inzaghi's teams could rarely compete on all fronts. Either they dug deep and dragged themselves ruthlessly through cup competitions, or they committed to domestic league dominance. Rarely did the two extremes meet.

In short, the experiences of the Milan clubs left a vacuum at the summit of Serie A. Throughout the 2010s, this vacuum was Juventus' to fill. The last time a league title had been won by a club outside of those three northern sides was 2000/01 when AS Roma claimed their third and latest Scudetto. This does not diminish Napoli's achievement. League titles are rarely won with rivals snapping at each other's heels until the very last round and, when they are, those seasons enter into folklore. There is something to be said for the collective psychology of a league when one side is so clearly superior to the rest: a communal sagging of the shoulders and rolling over for the belly to be tickled. In the 11 seasons between 2012/13 and 2022/23 there were seven instances of the Serie A winners being nine points or more ahead of their nearest rival. The drama and excitement of a 38-match campaign extends beyond just the title race. Relegation fears, European qualification battles, the nuances of improvement year on year or dramatic deterioration of a side's fortunes. However, the likelihood of a closely fought sprint for the crown is seldom seen, and one team's chokehold over the other 19 can't be dismissed on the basis of there being few to rival them.

Now that the external variables have been examined, the summer's recruitment and subsequent implementation of Luciano Spalletti's tactical plan can be detailed. Firstly, the importance of Cristiano Giuntoli should not be overlooked. Giuntoli became Napoli's sporting director in 2015/16 in the same summer that Maurizio Sarri replaced Rafael Benítez as manager. From that first season, Giuntoli had effectively regenerated the side three times.

The first wave of Giuntoli recruits brought Elseid Hysaj and Allan to Naples, then Akardiusz Milik and Piotr Zieliński. These shrewd signings offset the departure of Gonzalo Higuain, and built a side that finished second behind Juventus twice including an historic 91-point campaign (one point more than the title-winning team of 2022/23). Sarri departed, and Napoli's exceptional team was picked apart. Both Sarri and midfielder Jorginho left for Chelsea, and Napoli's all-time record appearance-maker Marek Hamšik followed suit in February 2019. By then, Giuntoli's rebuild had already begun.

Napoli made 11 transfers during the summer of 2018, and whilst not all successful or even recognisable to the untrained eye, all fit a specific profile. Only Orestis Karnezis, a Greek goalkeeper, and defender Kévin Malcut were aged 27 or older. Among the nine younger prospects were 21-year-old goalkeeper Alex Meret, signed from Udinese having never made a league appearance for the club, and young Spanish midfielder Fabián Ruiz for €30 million. Fabián's arrival was a statement not only financially but also in the player Napoli were acquiring. He had impressed at Real Betis as a two-way midfielder that offered creativity in attack and energy out of possession. There had been an explosion in this mould of player at the time. Frenkie De Jong had broken through at Ajax and was the talk of Europe, Giovani Lo Celso was signed by Real Betis to replace the Napoli-bound Fabián, and Tanguy Ndombélé would become Tottenham's all-time record transfer a year later. Vertical midfielders that could slice through the middle of the pitch and defy an opposition's press were in vogue, and Fabián was a part of this movement.

The second wave of Giuntoli signings was completed in 2019/20. Giovanni Di Lorenzo arrived from Empoli.

David Ospina was a free transfer from Arsenal, Eljif Elmas signed from Fenerbahçe, Amir Rrahmani moved from Verona, Stanislav Lobotka joined from Celta Vigo, and Hirving Lozano was bought from PSV Eindhoven for a pricey €42 million. This was by far Giuntoli's most lavish spending spree, but once again the targets fit a young profile with high potential. Ospina was the oldest of these signing at 30 years old, and the others would all play a crucial role in winning the title three years later. The difference this season was that there were no heartbreaking losses for these new arrivals to soothe. Giuntoli and Aurelio De Laurentiis were no longer firefighting or mitigating, but actively pursuing something greater.

That season was a traumatic one for many reasons. Chiefly, the Covid-19 pandemic ripped through Europe and paused all social and communal activity. The effects of those few months in the spring and summer of 2020 are still being felt now as clubs forfeited ticket revenue as stadiums closed. On the pitch, Napoli's rebuild slowed under Carlo Ancelotti and Gennaro Gattuso. Whilst Gattuso managed to secure a Coppa Italia trophy (the first silverware of Giuntoli's time in Naples), a seventh-place finish was extremely disappointing. The next season saw improvement with the team finishing fifth, but Napoli continued to be reliant on the older core of their side. Centre-back Kalidou Koulibaly and attackers Dries Mertens and Lorenzo Insigne were immovable objects within the Napoli side, and the younger, newer recruits around them had yet to step up and alleviate the workload.

That season had marked the start of Giuntoli's third wave, namely the arrival of Victor Osimhen for a club-record €70 million (within which were add-on fees and player exchanges, as mentioned in an earlier chapter). Osimhen had spent just one solitary season at Lille, but 13 goals and four assists in 25 Ligue 1 starts had been enough to widen the eyes of Europe's biggest clubs. The fee paid for the then 21-year-old was a colossal overpay, and a transfer that was viewed through suspicious eyes for the years that followed. However, in order for Napoli to fend off interest from richer and more alluring projects than their own, they broke their glass transfer ceiling to land Osimhen. Three separate injuries (including a serious shoulder dislocation sustained on international duty that kept him out for 15 domestic and international matches) disrupted his debut campaign in Naples. A return of 13 goal involvements in 16 Serie A starts was enough for Osimhen to show his potential if not the record-breaking arrival Napoli fans had hoped for.

A season later, Napoli's transfer activity was restricted by the effects of the pandemic and they paid for just one arrival as the loan for Matteo Politano became formalised into a permanent transfer. A loan move for André-Frank Zambo Anguissa was a huge success and convinced the club to sign the Cameroonian a year later, and a free transfer for the out-of-contract centre-back Juan Jesus was confirmed. This was also the season of Luciano Spalletti's arrival in Naples.

The story has already been told. Napoli started in electric fashion before fading and finishing third to the dismay of their fanbase. The pillars of *I Partenopei*'s side were removed as Koulibaly, Fabián, Mertens and Insigne all left. Those already disgruntled by Napoli's collapse in the spring of 2022 were now at blood-boiling levels, and the anger directly landed at Spalletti's and De Laurentiis' doors.

In the background, Cristiano Giuntoli was signing off on the completion of his third regeneration. If Giuntoli had made a speciality in signing top players before they blossomed (he and then-Atalanta sporting director Giovanni Sartori were arguably Italy's best exponents at this), then 2022/23 was his zenith, his final masterpiece. Out went the older players on high wages, and in came a raft of young, unrecognisable names to take their place. One can argue whether Giuntoli or Spalletti foresaw the immediate roles these players would have. Their impact was profound, as Khvicha Kvaratskhelia, Kim Min-jae, Mathías Oliveira, Zambo Anguissa (on a permanent deal), Tanguy Ndombélé, Giovanni Simeone and Giacomo Raspadori arrived for less than €50 million.

The masterpiece could only be appreciated once these players began playing together, and the potential of their collective became apparent. Giuntoli's gamble paid off and signed off eight years of work. However, whilst the summer of 2022's revolving door only furthers the credit and genius of Giuntoli's work, it is also fair to suggest that Napoli could have sold their star assets sooner and for more money. Kalidou Koulibaly is the example that irked Napoli fans the most, given that Napoli had staved off interest from European giants for years. The eventual sale of the Senegalese captain to Chelsea for €38 million was significantly lower than Manchester City's opening bid of €60 million back in 2020, a bid that was rejected. Giuntoli's recruitment could not be questioned, but Napoli had lost their ability to sell while a player's value was highest. Atalanta's Sartori, now at Bologna, was as ruthless a seller as he was shrewd at recruiting. Seeing a player tick towards 30 years old with their value rocketing, Sartori knows the benefit of selling such assets for enormous financial gain and then reinvesting in squad improvement. In recouping just €62 million for the sales of Koulibaly, Mertens, Insigne and Fabián, Giuntoli and Napoli had missed out on huge sales. Nevertheless, it is hard to argue that the Scudetto-winning team of 2022/23 did not have Cristiano Giuntoli's fingerprints all over it.

* * *

'Systems no longer exist in football, it's all about the spaces left by the opposition. You must be quick to spot them and know the right moment to strike, and have the courage to start the move even when pressed.'

Where many in football can struggle to articulate their vision and communicate it to the masses, Luciano Spalletti thrives. He is a romantic, perhaps created through a coaching career of developing sides to play stunning football without securing that coveted league title. He cares about his craft, and his craft is to play attacking football that not only wins, but makes supporters feel and love. The above quote is the perfect starting point when discussing Spalletti's tactical idea.

Spalletti's sides are nominally described in a 4-3-3 that morphs into a 4-2-1-3, a 4-1-4-1, and a 4-1-2-3. Realistically, the only time this 4-3-3 shape can be seen is on the tactical line-up display offered by the television broadcasters before the match. This is not to say that

Spalletti adopts total relationism and leaves the players to their own devices to form patterns and combinations. There is fluidity between these shapes, but they move according to predetermined instructions and roles that each player follows according to certain triggers on the pitch. Fluidity governed by strict rules and guidelines; an oxymoron but perhaps the best way to describe Spalletti's shifts in shape.

In possession Napoli looked like 2-1-4-3, a 3-4-3, or even a 3-3-4. As Spalletti himself says: 'It's all about spaces left by the opposition.' When playing out from goalkeeper Alex Meret, Napoli's modes of progression were to either totally dominate the ball with slow rotation across the defence to lure the opponent forward, or to snap past an opposition's press with quick interchanges and even a long and lofted pass upfield. The extreme duality to Napoli's game was what made them so tricky to tie down and create a gameplan for.

The first of those approaches is when Napoli would adopt the 3-4-3 in-possession shape as the full-backs pushed high and in line with the midfielders while Stanislav Lobotka dropped between the centre-backs. Regardless of the shape or tempo Napoli tried to instil, Lobotka was the crucial piece. In this scenario, Lobotka retreating into the defensive line gave Napoli enough bodies to rotate the ball and create angles, and thus afforded Giovanni Di Lorenzo the license to push further forward from right-back. Patiently moving the ball around, Napoli would creep forward to the point that they could encamp themselves on the halfway line and choke the other team inside their half. It can be argued that if this happened, then the opponent had done their job well and not allowed themselves to be sucked in and pulled out of shape. If they had, and a forward's eyes lit up at the prospect of robbing the ball high, then Lobotka and Kim Min-jae were able to quickly play a ball past them and advance up the pitch.

The role of Mario Ruí and Giovanni Di Lorenzo in this should not be overlooked. The former is a skilled enough ball-player to move back and contribute in deep build-up, and the latter is an archetypal modern full-back that offers a vertical running threat on the overlap. Each player's strengths assisted Napoli building out from the back in an asymmetrical shape with Di Lorenzo high and Mario Ruí either sinking back in line with the centre-backs (and thus allowing Lobotka to float between the lines and pick up the ball slightly ahead of the defenders), or remaining tight to the touchline to offer a consistent option to move the ball out wide.

They also allowed an even more aggressive and vertical option to be taken whereby Meret could knock the ball out to the full-backs himself and immediately move past the deepest phase of possession. Meret's short and medium passing was watertight, completing all 189 short passes played in the Serie A season and 99.3% of the 441 medium range passes in his 34 appearances. When Meret went long, usually straight to Victor Osimhen, the Italian could find his target 63.1% of the time. Inter's André Onana, hailed as one of the best ball-playing goalkeepers seen in the modern era, completed 54.7% of his long passes in the 2022/23 season.

Credit must be given to Osimhen for this as the Nigerian's strength and aerial flexibility could bring down balls from a great height, where other forwards might not be tall or powerful enough to gather. Meret's role in switching play from comfortably short, switching to the wings, and also launching high, presented a conundrum to opposition sides when deciding how they would pressure Napoli inside their half. While on the subject of Meret, his 16 clean sheets were only bettered by Lazio's Ivan Provedel, and his save rate of 74.7% was the league's third-best.

Meret was protected brilliantly by a diligent screening midfield and athletic, powerful centre-backs at the peaks of their powers. This meant that Meret was facing less than three shots on target per match and would often spend long periods without the ball coming near his goal. When called upon, Meret's presence was a reliable if unspectacular one. His Post-Shot xG (a metric that not only considers where the shot is taken from, but also its placement and the goalkeeper's positioning) of 25 was one greater than the 24 goals conceded, meaning that across the season Meret saved one more goal than he let in. In a team that plays on the halfway line and cuts out opposition attacks a long time before they reach the penalty area, this is the solid foundation required of a goalkeeper. Having only played seven matches in Spalletti's first season in Naples, Meret's contribution should be applauded.

While lots of possession was integral to Napoli's gameplan, they were not as choking nor relentless in their ball dominance as, for example, a Pep Guardiola team. In Spalletti's last five seasons in Serie A (from his sole season at Roma in 2016/17, two campaigns with Inter between 2017 and 2019, and then two year at Napoli), his teams had never posted below an average 57% possession. In fact, the last three (Inter 2018/19, Napoli 2021/22 and 2022/23) had seen Spalletti sides finish top of the possession rankings by the end of the season. The title-winning effort of 22/23 was his most ball-dominant, averaging 61.8% possession in that season.

However, this was not the product of safe circulation in the defensive third. The purpose was to shift quickly past the opposition press and occupy the middle and attacking thirds with lots of bodies. This is reflected in the numbers, whereby Napoli's 7,168 touches in the defensive third were the fourth-lowest in Serie A, ahead of only Fiorentina, Hellas Verona and Lecce. Move up the pitch by one third, and Napoli's 13,935 touches were not only the most but over 1,600 more than the next best (Lazio). Most of the heavy lifting on the ball was left to the Napoli back four positioned in the middle of the pitch, and Lobotka. In fact, five Napoli players featured inside the top ten for most touches in the 2022/23 season. Kim led the way, just shy of 200 touches clear of Giovanni Di Lorenzo, and followed by André-Frank Zambo Anguissa, Lobotka and Amir Rrahmani. All three of Di Lorenzo, Zambo Anguissa and Lobotka dictated matches with their attraction to the ball, both in playing lots of passes but also in breaking lines by carrying and dribbling. Kim also offered this threat as a powerful runner from deep, but his role was mostly to shift the ball around and offer a solid base from which Napoli's expressive and brilliant dribblers could turn possession into attacking transition.

The excellence of Kim's debut season in Naples can't be overstated. Stepping into the immense shoes of Kalidou Koulibaly, Kim was every bit as dominant defensively as the Senegalese and had greater attacking threat both on the ball and from set pieces. He may have played in the defensive line of the champions and the league's dominant force, but Kim's 123 clearances was the fourth-most in Serie A, whilst also tackling 86.3% of dribblers faced (the best that season) and finishing second for progressive carry distance (behind team-mate Rrahmani). Few players could beat Kim in a footrace, meaning Napoli were well protected should a ball be played in behind their high line, nor better combine sophisticated passing and carrying with dogged and at times brutal defensive work.

As the aggressor, Kim was the ball-winner and active defender. Rrahmani was his silent partner, defending space rather than attacking the ball whilst also offering incisive carrying in possession. As mentioned earlier, the Kosovan carried the ball for more progressive yards than any player in Serie A across the 22/23 season. Kim's 96 tackles and interceptions were more than double Rrahmani's 47, and the South Korean's 145 contested aerial duels dwarfed the 107 of his partner (notably, both won more than 62% of these duels). Perhaps the best statistical representation of the contrast between the pair was in their clearances: 123 for Kim, 79 for Rrahmani. These metrics can be caveated by Kim having played 500 more minutes in Serie A than Rrahmani, but nevertheless the scale of difference between the pair went beyond the numbers, the rambunctiousness of Kim, both defensively and on the ball, counterbalanced by Rrahmani's work in the shadows. The dog chases, the cat patrols.

Once camped on the halfway line or away from the defensive third, Napoli's combinations could take shape. Assuming Stanislav Lobotka had driven play from the back into midfield, there were options across many angles for him to find. Di Lorenzo and Mario Ruí might find themselves hugging the touchline or tucked in close to Lobotka. Zambo Anguissa and Piotr Zieliński would be pushed ahead of Lobotka in the half-spaces between the wingers and middle of the pitch. Then there were the wide attackers, stationed high and as wide as they could possibly go. Lobotka was the perfect player to make the right decision in these instances.

Time moved differently for Napoli's No. 68, easing out of the way of more physical players to shift momentum forward. Spalletti likened him to the great Spanish midfielder Andrés Iniesta for this reason, as both could dribble their way out of impossible situations using incredible balance and weight of touch before finding the perfect pass. Often this would see Lobotka play a pass into the wide forwards, taking out opposition players in the process but also freeing space for Zambo Anguissa and Zieliński to make a run forward away from the ball's distraction. Lobotka was the heartbeat of Spalletti's team, a portal through which everything passed and all that came after could be traced back to. The Slovenian was the culmination of Spalletti's honing of the *regista*, dating back to his transformation of David Pizarro nearly 20 years before at Udinese.

Lobotka was not the only excellent ball carrier in that midfield. Zambo Anguissa and Zieliński could both dribble and shift an attack's dynamic with the ball at their feet, although Zieliński's greatest asset was his movement and willingness to join the attack in and out of possession. When asked which player personified Napoli's success,

Patrick Kendrick named the Pole. 'Zieliński was essentially the only real survivor of the Maurizio Sarri crop and he allowed Spalletti to field a 4-3-3 that morphed into a 4-2-3-1.' In Zieliński's seven seasons at the club, only once had he scored fewer than his three goals in 2022/23. However, his eight assists were the second-best of his Napoli career, and 5.31 shot-creating actions per 90 minutes (participating in one of the two actions that directly led to a shot) was a huge increase on the previous season (3.96). Interestingly, Zieliński had scored twice as many goals in 2021/22, but these numbers show that his overall involvement in chance creation and role in possession had changed from Spalletti's first season.

Napoli's number 99 was arguably their most eye-catching player outside of Khvicha Kvaratskhelia and Victor Osimhen. André-Frank Zambo Anguissa is a rare breed of midfielder that can accelerate from languid and laid-back to devastating and powerful in the space of seconds. His strength had always been as a ball carrier, dropping the shoulder and using incredible upper-body strength to manoeuvre away from opponents; and the Cameroonian would seemingly thrive in inviting pressure with his back to goal before changing direction and slaloming 180 degrees in the opposite direction. Zambo Anguissa had long been a player to enjoy on YouTube highlights reels, if not at the very best clubs.

The 2022/23 season saw a different side to Zambo Anguissa. Luciano Spalletti had seemingly coaxed out a new side to his game that elevated him to a new level. The carrying and dribbling remained but there was now an added threat as an off-ball runner and as a dictator from deep. Zambo Anguissa's 1,988 completed passes that season were over 400 more than in any season of his career since 2017, and those passes progressed play by a total of 28,244 yards. This was over 8,000 yards more than in any other campaign as Zambo Anguissa's passing improved significantly. Then there was his attacking threat; 1.48 shots per 90 minutes is far from groundbreaking but it was half a shot more than in his previous season. His three goals in Serie A represented his best-ever return, and eight assists across all competitions account for more than half of his 15 at club level.

This was a new and improved André-Frank Zambo Anguissa, one that not only could slice a team open with powerful carrying, but could also sit on the ball and play in a team-mate with a pass or make a third-man run into the penalty area to score himself. Then there was his off-ball diligence. When Napoli shifted to their out of possession shape, Zambo Anguissa and Lobotka would routinely find themselves man-marking the opposition's central midfielders and cutting out passes into them. Zambo Anguissa intercepted 49 passes in the 2022/23 season; the most of any Napoli player and eighth-most overall in Serie A. If Napoli's Scudetto win saw the elevation of individuals above any level they had seen in their career, then Zambo Anguissa's transformation could be the most impressive.

With the midfielders and full-backs interchanging in tight triangles and overloading the opposition team, Napoli's forwards had little involvement. That is until the wingers were engaged, namely Kvaratskhelia. On the right, Matteo Politano and Hirving Lozano offered a more nuanced threat. Politano presented a more cultured option, dropping deeper and allowing Giovanni Di Lorenzo to overlap by dragging the full-back with him. A repeating move, as observed by *The Athletic*'s Liam Tharme, is one sequence where Politano would collect the ball from a centre-back as Di Lorenzo bombed past him. Politano, a naturally left-footed player, would swing a first-time pass over the top for Di Lorenzo or Osimhen to chase in the space he had vacated. This was useful against teams that would sit deep and try and reduce the space rather than attack Napoli, as Politano's movement could free up precious space for Di Lorenzo and Osimhen to venture into.

Against more able opponents, Lozano's pace and threat in transition was valuable. The Mexican's speed across the ground was lethal against teams that attacked Napoli high, such as in the Champions League or against rivals at the top of the division. The pair split their minutes evenly as Spalletti rotated and interchanged them according to the match situation, and at least one of them started in 34 of the 38 league matches. It was arguably the position of most change across the season as Eljif Elmas also slotted in on the right during Napoli's injury-hit winter, but 12 goals and assists from Politano and Lozano reflect their impact on the team and contributions at different points in the season.

So, the ball is shifted right. Politano swings a pass over his marker for Giovanni Di Lorenzo to speed on to and cut back, or Hirving Lozano runs at the opponent and clips a cross centrally for Victor Osimhen. But what happened when the ball went left, and not right? What happened was bringing the 2022/23 Serie A MVP into the match.

Khvicha Kvaratskhelia would start wide with chalk on his boots from positioning himself on the touchline. Doing so stretched the opposition before he even had the ball as they sought to negate his threat. Kvaratskhelia could hurt an opposition in many ways. One was to cut inside and crack powerful shots at goal with his laces or whip with his instep. Bringing the ball centrally was not just a means to shooting goalwards, however. Kvaratskhelia's 2.97 shots per 90 minutes is lower than one imagines when they picture a firecracker winger of his ilk. Carrying the ball inside brought Piotr Zieliński back into play as the advanced midfielder on the left. These two players, with Mario Ruí tucked close, formed a connection across the season that few could handle; cute one-twos, giving-and-going with one-touch passes and swapping positions to confuse their markers. Much is said of Kvaratskhelia benefitting from the threat of Victor Osimhen centrally, but Zieliński's role as the closest midfielder was critical in feeding Kvaratskhelia both the ball and space.

The other option Kvaratskhelia could take was to feed Mario Ruí on the overlap and wait for the ball back as opposition players were sucked out by the left-back. A quick look up and a swing of that right boot would send the ball in for Osimhen to attack. Then there was Kvaratskhelia's threat down the outside, blistering past a full-back and getting close to the byline to cross low. Like the very best wingers, Khvicha Kvaratskhelia was not restricted to one mode of attack.

A quick dip into the Georgian's numbers reflect one of the greatest debut seasons a player has had in one of Europe's top-five leagues: 12 goals and 13 assists (inflated by just two penalty kicks) in Serie A and 14 goals and 17 assists in 43 appearances across all competitions. Only Rafael Leão could come close to Kvaratskhelia's carrying into the penalty area and even he attempted 20 fewer. The breadth of Kvaratskhelia's attacking involvement can be seen in his shot- and goal-creating action figures. His 0.86 topped Serie A for goal-creating actions per 90 minutes (participating in at least one of the two actions directly before a goal) and he had the eighth-highest shot-creating actions per 90 minutes in the league (4.86). In other words, Kvaratshkelia was involved in nearly five of Napoli's 15.92 shots per 90 minutes, and performed an action in creating or scoring a goal just under once a match. These were creative figures that only the very best attain, let alone a 22-year-old in his maiden season in Italy.

To fully understand and describe Kvaratskhelia's brilliance, one must include his relationship with Victor Osimhen. Kvaratskhelia assisted six of Osimhen's 26 Serie A goals in 2022/23 as the pair fed off each other's strengths. The archetypal Kvaratskhelia–Osimhen link-up saw the Georgian cut inside from the left and clip crosses to the back post where Osimhen would rise and head goalwards. Take Osimhen's goal in the thrashing of Juventus as an example. Kvaratskhelia's cross is delivered with perfect whip, wedged off his instep to move through the air with speed and land perfectly on Osimhen's head. It bisects the Juventus centre-backs and Osimhen guides the header home. There were other combinations too. Delicate through-passes that allowed Osimhen to run on to a moving ball and finish, low crosses fired into the Nigerian's feet, and simple tee-ups too. Theirs was a partnership so potent that their fates are forever bound in the image of 2022/23. They will forever be Kvaratskhelia AND Osimhen.

Finally, there was Osimhen himself, Serie A's top scorer and the first African player to ever win the *capocannoniere*: 26 goals in Serie A, 31 in all competitions in 2022/23. The ingredients of a world-class striker had always been there: the raw pace, power and strength, the flexibility to reach balls few could, the powerful ball-striking, and the abundant charisma and personality. His 14 goals in 2021/22 had hinted that the volcano was about to erupt, with the underlying numbers pointing towards a star in the making. Over four shots per 90 minutes and underperforming his xG in just two of the last four seasons was enough to convince onlookers of his potential. His shots per 90 minutes increased by 0.5 in the following campaign, his shot accuracy leapt up by nearly 8%, and the average distance of shot dropped to 12.8 yards (the lowest of Osimhen's career). In other words, Osimhen was shooting more frequently, more accurately, and from much closer than at any point since moving to France in 2019. This was the fully moulded Osimhen, combining clinical finishing and reliability both in front of goal and in being fit to start 30 out of 38 Serie A matches, with the added frills of scoring some of the season's defining goals. The pair against Roma home and away sum up the brilliance of Osimhen; one came from chasing a long ball into the channel before thumping a shot home from an impossible angle, whilst the other was brought down from a ridiculous height and hit equally hard into the roof of the net. In a new era of centre-forward excellence, supercharged by the likes of Erling Haaland and Harry Kane, Osimhen put himself firmly at the entrance door to that elite group with his exploits in 2022/23.

Even a team as brilliant on the ball as Napoli require a sophisticated structure when out of possession. Their time out of possession was the lowest by percentage in Serie A, and so their defensive numbers alone are not enough to illustrate what their approach was. Only Sassuolo and Torino won fewer tackles than Napoli in the league, but no side attempted more tackles in the final third than their 106. This demonstrates Luciano Spalletti's out of possession mantra: if the ball is lost high up the pitch, turn it into an attacking opportunity. One of the automatisms Spalletti coached into his Napoli side to do this was to press high in a 4-4-2, or even a 4-2-4. The wingers would shadow their opposing full-back, and Osimhen would be joined by Zieliński to close down the centre-backs should the ball be played short from the goalkeeper. The objective is not necessarily to win the ball here, but to force a mistake or a long pass that can then be swept up by Kim and Rrahmani, and Napoli's possession phase could begin again.

When pressing in this way, Zieliński is required to retreat very quickly and rejoin the midfield should the press be broken or played through. Few players can perform this extremely energetic role off the ball, but the Pole's work rate and engine are every bit as impressive as his high technical level. It would become apparent how crucial this role was when Zieliński was absent and Tanguy Ndombélé played. The Frenchman lacked the speed and awareness to cover the ground like Zieliński, and Napoli's press would suffer as a result.

Emphasis lay on Kim and Rrahmani to maintain a high line and not be forced backwards. A high press can only work if the defensive line also pushes high and squeezes the opposition into a congested central area. Failure to do so would leave wide open spaces for an opponent to run through should they skip past the first line of pressure. In cramping opposition teams in this way, Napoli's combative central midfielders were given a better chance at cutting out passes and turning possession over, or winning the ball back in the tackle.

As explained earlier, Zambo Anguissa ranked inside the top ten for interceptions, and Lobotka's 44 successful tackles were the most by any Napoli player. Between them and the tireless Zieliński, Napoli were able to strip possession quickly and feed their explosive forward line without relying on Kvaratskhelia or Osimhen to defend too actively.

Throughout Luciano Spalletti's career, he had strived for a team as complete and functional as this, one that could perform his tactical demands perfectly without losing sight of playing fearless, beautiful football. Roma had often been too emotional, unable to detach themselves from the occasion and capable of implosion. On a tactical level, his first stint there was so heavily reliant on Francesco Totti and David Pizarro that nullifying the pair went a long way to beating Roma. At Inter he had lacked creativity from wide and goalscorers to share the load with Mauro Icardi. Even his first Napoli side lacked the ruthlessness of his 2022/23 team, and did not have the bite, energy or tempo-setting capabilities he imprinted on to them in his second season.

This was a team that could move from the patient and cautious to full-throttle attack in the skip of a heartbeat, that was smart and drilled enough to float between shapes without losing sight of individual roles and responsibilities, and one that promoted individual decision-making within a structured system. It was a team that Eintracht Frankfurt coach Oliver Glasner described as 'anti-Italian' and 'very aggressive'. Followers of Serie A in recent years will know that the stereotype of Italian football being slow and defensive was outdated and failed to reflect the stunning football played by the teams of Spalletti, Gian Piero Gasperini, Roberto De Zerbi and Thiago Motta to name but a few. However, Spalletti's Napoli rose above the cynical European view of Serie A football and ignited interest from beyond Italy.

Within weeks of the season starting and Napoli hitting their devastating peak, players like Kvaratskhelia, Osimhen, Kim and Lobotka were being discussed in hushed tones across the continent to an even greater extent than Champions League finalists Inter's star players. There is a case that Napoli under Spalletti had the greatest impact on football fans around Europe of any Italian side since the days of Juventus under Antonio Conte, when Paul Pogba, Arturo Vidal and Andrea Pirlo formed one of the great modern midfields in the early 2010s.

The Farm

THERE IS an infectiousness to Luciano Spalletti's interviews and press conference appearances. Dressed casually in club merchandise tracksuit, Spalletti rides through media interrogation with confidence and performance. Wry smiles, the odd wink of the eye, responding to the question by addressing the journalist personally, and a casual shrug of the shoulders while slowly winding down an avenue of metaphors and analogies. Many end exactly where he started; his farm in rural Tuscany.

With these idiosyncrasies in mind, little seemed awry in the coach's press briefing on Sunday, 21 May. His title-winning Napoli had just dispatched an in-form Inter side 3-1. Rather than one of overwhelming celebration, there was uncertainty and mystery. This was the result of chairman Aurelio De Laurentiis' recent comments concerning Spalletti's future in Naples. As Napoli cruised towards the Scudetto and advanced in peerless fashion through the Champions League rounds, questions had begun to be asked to De Laurentiis about whether Spalletti would be awarded a new contract to extend his stay. The two-year deal he was awarded upon joining in 2021 now looked remarkably short, but there was little concern about whether he would remain. At the very least, the option to extend by a further year looked a nailed-on certainty. Spalletti was happy, the team was winning, and De Laurentiis was satisfied.

So satisfied, that the president opted to activate the extension clause in Spalletti's contract. That Spalletti had not been consulted about such a decision seemed academic to De Laurentiis. Hopefully, this book will have painted an all-encompassing portrait of Spalletti's character and personality: a principled and traditional man with strong values and great humour, but also one with a bite and edge that keeps his head above the parapet of messy intra-club relationships. We may never know whether Spalletti truly intended on staying another year in Naples. The signs were there that he would extend potentially by two further years, and such news was being reported right up until the week of the victory over Inter.

As it was, Spalletti was disappointed by De Laurentiis' presumptive action. For all he had achieved at Napoli that season, Spalletti maintained his dignity and professional integrity above almost all else. He was not a pawn in De Laurentiis' operation, to be controlled and dictated to. This was his team, and his club. So when the chairman was asked routinely throughout the spring about his coach's future, and responded with affirming statements of a looming extension, Spalletti held firm in his convictions. 'He should be telling that to me, not you,' was his answer.

James Horncastle detailed the breakdown of the relationship in a beautiful article for *The Athletic*. In it, he described the scene at a famous Neapolitan restaurant where Spalletti and De Laurentiis discussed out the situation over a typically stunning dinner. This meeting has now become the stuff of folklore, and the site where Spalletti confirmed his intention to leave Napoli. He had hinted at such a decision through cryptic references to the dinner, informing journalists that his decision had been made over the table and that 'This is not something that just fell out of the sky from nowhere.' (*Football Italia*).

There were technicalities to the divorce too. The suspected plunder of his team following their exceptional individual and collective season could not be ignored, even through the most wishful of sky blue lenses. De Laurentiis had emphasised that offers for the likes of Victor Osimhen and Khvicha Kvaratskhelia could be turned down, and that pressure from Premier League clubs to sell would be denied. Yet the possibility of losing multiple parts of the side remained real. For Spalletti, a coach that first and foremost looks to work and improve the players at his disposal, this in itself would not have broken his resolve. This reality was paired with Juventus' public pursuit of sporting director Cristiano Giuntoli. Credited with being the driving force behind the acquisitions of the two aforementioned stars, plus Kim Min-jae and numerous others since assuming the role in 2015, Giuntoli had given Napoli an edge in scouting and recruitment that ultimately powered them to the Serie A title. Were he to be tempted to the Old Lady, then success would have come at great cost to Napoli.

These details are important in assessing the shock departure of Luciano Spalletti. However, the actions of De Laurentiis remained the ultimate betrayal to Spalletti, and the deciding factor in his exit. It is not the first time he has left a club on the highest of notes. In 2005 he departed Udinese just days after guiding them to the Champions League. His second stint at Roma ended after just a season, in which they finished on a club record 87 points. Relationships within the club and the publicised souring of matters with Francesco Totti left Spalletti feeling disrespected by his employers. There is something to be said for Spalletti knowing when his time is done, and not outstaying his welcome. He said as much in the press conference on 21 May 2023, saying: 'If you are not convinced you can give everything these people deserve, it's right to think it [his position] over. You think it over, you arrive at a conclusion and then you stick with it.'

The character of the man plays a huge part in understanding why he chose to leave. As Napoli bruised their way to the Champions League quarter-finals, their path to the final in Istanbul became clear if not yet secure. A quarter-final with an out-of-form Milan side would precede a semi-final against either Inter or Benfica, and then the real possibility of facing one of Real Madrid, Bayern Munich or Manchester City in the final. Their form, and the intensity of good feeling around the club, caused many to even tip them to win the competition altogether.

City manager Pep Guardiola was asked about their chances and the strength of their case despite having little-to-no experience in the deeper stages against sides of this quality. 'Against Napoli I do not want to talk as their manager will be grumpy with me. He's so sensitive,' laughed Guardiola. Spalletti's bristling demeanour precedes him, and was no doubt exaggerated by the recent exploits of fellow Italian coaches Roberto De Zerbi and Cristian Stellini in an explosive touchline altercation at Tottenham Hotspur Stadium. As explained in previous chapters, Spalletti is from a traditional school of Italian managers that place respect and professional integrity at the forefront of everything they do.

De Laurentiis' back-tracking had already begun at this point, stating that he did not intent to 'clip wings' by begging with Spalletti to stay. It turned out to be the perfect framing of the situation. At 64 years old, Spalletti's intentions were clear. Rather than leap from the bedlam and emotional roller coaster that is living in Naples (let alone managing their football team), he sought a return to his farm. 'As for what I'm going to do, I don't need wings for it,' said Spalletti, referencing De Laurentiis' attempts to twist the narrative into Spalletti outgrowing his surroundings. 'I need a pair of Wellington boots.'

Once his resignation had been formalised and publicly announced, there was time for one more heartfelt moment between Naples and Spalletti. On his final day at the club training centre, the group of ultras who had stolen his car back in October 2021 presented Spalletti with a gift box, tied with a bow. Inside was the steering wheel that they had returned the car without, from which Spalletti took great amusement. It demonstrated how far the relationship had come, from those days of scepticism bordering on harassment towards Spalletti, to being sent on his way with a humorous parting gift to say thank you.

Naples is not the sort of city to be quickly moved on from. It embeds itself within the soul. The smells, the noise, the feverish excitement and pace of life and passion of its people. It would have been impossible for Spalletti to leap straight back on to the management carousel and land another role so quickly after Napoli.

That left just one place for Spalletti to return to: the farm.

* * *

It takes a special kind of mettle to be Napoli's coach. For one, it takes special character to live in Naples, let alone manage its football club. There are so many conflating factors involved. There is the history and lore. The figure of Maradona hangs over every player to ever have played, but a deity like that looms even larger when representing Napoli. His achievements made the club what it is, but his cult of personality was so deeply intertwined with Naples that one must respect and treasure the traditions and history he created. His name is repeated at every press conference, his face on flags and walls of the city. You are not only managing Napoli, nor just Naples. You are the custodian of Maradona's team. That carries its own weight that few can handle.

Then there is the weight of expectation for a generation that was built off the back of Maradona's Napoli and restoring the current iterations to similar glories. Now, the new coach and successor to Luciano Spalletti would have to pick up the baton of the first side to break their drought. There is a serious debate to be had about whether any future Scudetto, for at least the foreseeable future, could ever emulate the outpouring of emotion generated by Spalletti's title. So heavy was the legacy, and so cumbersome was the slumber, that the 2022/23 Serie A title became far greater than a mere footballing achievement. How could anything follow that, with the exception of perhaps European titles?

Then there were the more granular matters of inner-club drama. As hopefully outlined in these pages, Aurelio De Laurentiis is far from the easiest executive in football to work with. His work in rebuilding Napoli from the ruins to an elite, title-winning side can't be ignored nor sneered at. However, his reputation for bolshie power plays within the boardroom and public arguments with managers offsets such success. It also makes the prospect of working with him a less-than-appealing one. All these influences against the backdrop of potential widespread squad turnover meant that the Napoli job remained one of the toughest in European football, even when the squad in question had just won a title.

Rumoured candidates covered the entire football spectrum in all of style, personality, age and feasibility. Within Serie A, Fiorentina's Vincenzo Italiano was heavily linked following impressive stints at Spezia and *I Viola*, and having taken the latter to the Europa Conference League Final in 2023. His style was ambitious and possession-heavy, and he was young enough to represent the start of a long-term project. Gian Piero Gasperini was also linked. The then 65-year-old certainly matched Spalletti's prickly temperament and aggressive philosophy, but the Atalanta coach's long-running feud with Neapolitans made this an unlikely marriage. Luis Enrique had recently left his post as Spain manager, and his reputation remained stratospheric even eight years after winning a treble with Barcelona in 2015. Julian Nagelsmann had been ruthlessly sacked by Bayern Munich, and again ticked the boxes of youth (still only 35 at the time or writing) and exhilarating, fluid attacking football. Antonio Conte, whose most recent managerial stint at Tottenham Hotspur had ended in the usual catherine wheel of explosive accusation and finger-pointing one has come to expect, also later commented that he had held conversations over the vacancy.

Any of the four named would have been intriguing choices for their own reasons. None were appointed. Instead, as the weeks drew on and each of the candidates committed to their existing roles (Italiano and Gasperini) or joined new projects (Enrique was hired by Paris Saint-Germain), the shortlist narrowed. The new hire was no longer set to be a high-profile name to energise the squad and use the momentum generated by the previous season. It was now a case of finding a candidate to steady a rocking ship, destabilised by the waves of De Laurentiis' and Spalletti's fracas and a quickly changing squad.

Rudi Garcia had not been a name mentioned readily by Napoli fans. Interestingly, he and Spalletti had reversed the roles of predecessor and successor in 2016 when Garcia's three-year tenure at AS Roma ended and Spalletti replaced him. This chain of events saw Spalletti achieve a monumental 87 points and second-place finish before walking away in a now-familiar manner. Just three seasons before, Garcia had taken the club to second place with 85 points and followed it with another second-place finish. So Spalletti's success was not framed against the failures of a previous regime, but rather extending its work. Now, it was time for Garcia to reverse the roles.

There is plenty to admire and appreciate about Garcia's managerial career. Those three years in Rome had featured highly impressive moments, even if Spalletti had followed him and turned a stagnating side into a free-flowing attacking force. His three seasons at Marseille that followed were unspectacular, and a brief spell at Lyon was also uninspiring beyond a run to the semi-finals of the Champions League in 2019/20. Before Napoli, he had been a manager in Saudi Arabia with Al-Nassr. His departure in April 2023 came before the flurry of transfer activity in the summer of 2023 that elevated the league's status beyond what many thought possible.

Upon his unveiling before Napoli's pre-season fixtures in mid-July, Garcia thanked Spalletti. He stated that the team and city he walked into was 'full of smiles, joy and enthusiasm'. Now it was Garcia's job to maintain such an atmosphere and continue the work of Spalletti before him. The first major change to manage was Kim Min-jae's transfer to Bayern Munich for €50m. The South Korean's rise had been meteoric, having only moved to Europe in 2021 by joining Fenerbahçe of Turkey. In just two years Kim had scaled the heights of European football, winning a Serie A title and now joining the German champions. It is a story and ascent few can match, and it also represented the first of Spalletti's Scudetto winners to depart Naples.

The other major casualty that summer was Hirving Lozano, who returned to PSV Eindhoven, his previous club. The Mexican had shared the right-wing spot with Matteo Politano throughout the title-winning campaign, and whilst six goal involvements in 33 league appearances might not sound like a decisive impact, his role was crucial. Lozano's pace and directness kept opposition defences honest, and his commitment in helping lead the press off the ball would be difficult to replicate. Sharing attacking duties with Osimhen and Kvaratskhelia required an ego-less mould of player, one that would be happy to see less of the ball than his more esteemed team-mates and work tirelessly without it. For this, Lozano was perfect.

Kim and Lozano aside, the squad suffered very few outgoings. Victor Osimhen had been subject to intense media speculation surrounding a €150m move to the Premier League, Paris Saint-Germain or Saudi Arabia depending on which newspaper you were reading that day. Garcia supposedly held talks with the forward and warned him that a move to Saudi Arabia would be ill-advised. The irony, in Garcia having recently coached and been sacked from the very same Saudi Arabian league, should not be lost. It was the first in a string of Osimhen-related blunders that would come to define Garcia's Napoli tenure.

Khvicha Kvaratskhelia was also continually linked with a move away from Naples off the back of his remarkable breakthrough season. It was widely believed that Napoli would cash in on one of their prized attacking assets, and keep the other for another season. To the delight of their fans, and no doubt Garcia, Napoli managed to retain both Osimhen and Kvaratskhelia for the 2023/24 season. If Garcia was ever going to make his mark at the club, this pair were his best chance.

Napoli's additions were intriguing, if not the marquee names nor profiles ready to immediately shoulder the burden of the shirt and the preceding season. Kim's replacement was Natan, a raw 21-year-old centre-back signed from Red Bull Bragantino. The midfield was bolstered with the arrivals of Jens Cajuste from Stade de Reims and the highly regarded Jesper Lindstrom of Eintracht Frankfurt. Giacomo Raspadori and Giovanni Simeone, both loanees during the title triumph, had their transfers made permanent too.

The stage was set for the trickiest of assignments possible. Napoli were defending their Scudetto without the beloved coach who took them to their promise land. Away at Frosinone in their new kit flecked with accents of gold, Victor Osimhen began the season where he had left off in the previous one. Despite Napoli going behind to the newly promoted *I Canarini*, the Nigerian lashed a brace to add to Matteo Politano's first-half equaliser, giving Garcia his maiden Napoli victory. They followed this opening-day victory with another, at home to Sassuolo, before a disappointing 2-1 home loss to Lazio. This defeat, at the hands of former Napoli manager Maurizio Sarri, set alarm bells ringing. Despite hogging nearly two-thirds of possession against a side that themselves enjoy dominating the ball, Napoli lacked their cutting edge. Osimhen and Kvaratskhelia took a combined 11 shots in the match; only one found the target in a profligate showing.

The worst was yet to come. Five points from meetings with Genoa, Braga and Bologna does not read terribly on paper, but the nature of the performances pointed to troubled waters. Napoli went behind for the third time in four matches in a 2-2 draw with Genoa and required interventions from the in-form pair of Raspadori and Politano to draw level. Opening night in the Champions League presented the familiar issue of a misfiring Osimhen. An astonishing nine efforts on goal were taken by the

2022/23 *capocannionere* winner without reward. An 88th-minute Braga own goal saved their blushes in a competition they had set alight one year previously. However, the goalless draw with Bologna sank things lower still. With the match locked at 0-0, Garcia substituted Osimhen in the 86th minute for Giovanni Simeone. Osimhen had earlier missed a penalty, but naturally remained Napoli's greatest threat in searching for a winner. Walking off the field, a furious Osimhen held two fingers up to his manager. Rather than cursing Garcia, Osimhen was seemingly demanding that both he and Simeone should be on the pitch and play as a pair. Visual displays of friction between a new manager and star player are hard to ignore. The pressure was ramping up on Garcia before October had even begun.

Osimhen's time on the front pages was not finished there. Following his missed penalty against Bologna, Napoli's TikTok account posted a bizarre video mocking the striker's miss with a high-pitched 'Gimme penalty please' audio. This followed an even more offensive post likening Osimhen to 'a coconut' just days before. A ridiculously avoidable situation had been created by the club's social media team, and threatened to completely destroy Osimhen's relationship with Napoli. The player's agent proposed legal action, and Osimhen himself deleted every Napoli-related post from his Instagram account; no break-up is complete in the modern internet age without such an act.

The standard of social media management by Serie A clubs leaves much to desired especially when compared with their Premier League rivals. In a time when many regard Serie A to be the second-best league in Europe, their ability to self-sabotage and diminish their brand via incoherent, insensitive or simply offensive content will forever hold them back. Napoli are a symptom of this, not the cause. Isolating and offending their star player was the nadir of a taxing period for the club. Neither they nor Garcia ever recovered. Time sought to soothe the tensions between them and Osimhen but the disconnect between the coach and his players was now glaringly obvious.

Kvaratskhelia had been substituted in September's draw with Genoa with the Georgian showing a similar level of disdain as Osimhen. Matteo Politano too, debatably Napoli's most consistent player in a turbulent season, was bemused at being removed in a 1-3 loss to Fiorentina. The rot had set in. Players were dissenting en masse, and Garcia's control was gone. One could argue that authority had never been established, dating back to his first weeks in the role when he publicly pondered over retaining Giovanni Di Lorenzo as club captain. Like so much that followed, this was an unnecessary and needless complication that set Garcia off on the wrong foot.

Club president Aurelio De Laurentiis remained steadfast in his support. Two international breaks came and went with Garcia still clinging to his job, until a 1-0 home defeat to Empoli in November in an insipid display. The time had come and, with Conte murmuring in the background, Garcia was removed from his post. Napoli had taken 22 points from their first 12 Serie A matches; ten points less than at the same stage in 2022/23.

On the day of this book's submission, Conte was all but confirmed by reliable sources as the new Napoli manager ahead of the 2024/25 season. Whether his pragmatic and transition-based 3-4-3 will translate to this group of players remains to be seen. The four-time Serie A champion's record is up there with the best, even if it yields immediate results at the expense of the long term. Rudi Garcia's dismissal was not followed by Conte's announcement, but the return of a familiar face. A decade on from his successful spell in Naples, Walter Mazzarri was appointed to stand on the touchline once again, a safe pair of hands to guide Napoli through to the end of the season.

Like Conte, Mazzarri is a steadfast believer in playing a three-man defence and so his appointment raised eyebrows from a tactical perspective as much as it did from any other. Having clearly observed Garcia's shortcomings, Mazzarri announced a new approach based around recapturing the magic created by Luciano Spalletti. In his first press appearance as Napoli manager, Mazzarri described Napoli as 'the strongest team I have ever coached' and a 'masterpiece created with Spalletti'. So enamoured with his new project was Mazzarri that he even ditched his 3-5-2 principles to play in Spalletti's 4-3-3. The sentiment was exactly what fans needed to hear.

That sentiment could only last so long. Under Mazzarri, Napoli won just four matches in three months. Only three times did they score more than once in a match, and there was a rotten run of three matches in a row without scoring. De Laurentiis swung the axe again as Napoli sat in ninth position and turned to a trusted former member of Spalletti's coaching staff. Francesco Calzona had worked under Spalletti during the 2021/22 season and left the club to become Slovakia national team coach at the end of that campaign. He would straddle the twin workload of national and international management for the duration of the 2023/24 season with the view of stepping aside from Napoli at the end of the campaign.

The lift of a familiar face on the touchline still could not touch the miserable form that had engulfed the team. Calzona won just three of 14 matches in charge, with the only saving grace being the uptick in Victor Osimhen's form. So poor had Napoli been that there would have been concerns that Osimhen's value had sunk as a result and with the Nigerian almost certain to leave, Napoli needed every extra euro they could extract from their talisman's sale. One year on from lifting the Scudetto, with the streets of Naples ground to a halt by the widespread delirium of winning the title, Napoli were booed off the pitch on the final day of the 2023/24 season. A 0-0 draw with Lecce confirmed a tenth-place finish: the worst title defence in Italy during the three-points-for-a-win era. To many, Napoli winning Serie A had been an event to stop the earth spinning on its axis. Their defence of that title was every bit as remarkable for all the wrong reasons.

It was unthinkable that a defending champion could defend their title so meekly: that a truly great side, one that could hold its own in a conversation surrounding the best of the last few decades, could follow up their crowning glory with such a dismal display.

From top to bottom, Napoli imploded. The managerial situation had proved laughable, and was perfectly summed up on 7 December 2023. Spalletti was officially awarded honorary citizenship of Naples for his role in Napoli's great success. It is an honour bestowed on the most beloved of managers in Italy, and often those that have had a reach far beyond football. For example, the northern city of Bergamo granted Atalanta coach Gian Piero Gasperini citizenship in 2019. The awkward situation arose of both Spalletti and Aurelio De Laurentiis attending the ceremony and being seen together for the first time since their acrimonious split. Both had been vocal in recalling their side of the story, and De Laurentiis had gone as far as to downplay Spalletti's part in the Scudetto win. Yet here they were, in person and celebrating Spalletti's contribution to Naples.

De Laurentiis' public remonstrations felt ever sharper and more toe-curling. Just weeks after Rudi Garcia's departure, the club president stated that he had not only held on too long to his coach, but that he should have sacked the coach on his first day in the role. This was the final twist of the knife in the Garcia–De Laurentiis saga, which had earlier included episodes such as the president entering the dressing room at half-time in matches against Milan and Union Berlin. De Laurentiis has never been one to shy away from the media spotlight, perhaps a by-product of his role in the film industry. Very few managers have ever left Naples without feeling his wrath, but the vocal disgracing of Garcia felt like a new nadir in the relations between club and coach. When the results are favourable, Aurelio De Laurentiis takes much of the credit. However, when the tables are turned, his tendency is to distance himself from the root causes and instead pour fuel on the fire (from within the house).

'Luciano Spalletti's departure was the most farcical of any coach under De Laurentiis,' says Kaustubh Pandey. 'Spalletti seemed keen on turning Napoli into an established European giant after winning the Scudetto. Judging by how things were going, he could have done that too, if the key players had stayed and the right investment was made.'

The overriding sense was that of a wasted opportunity. De Laurentiis had craved the thought of lifting the Serie A title as Napoli president, and yet within a year that memory had to battle the farce that followed. For Spalletti, he left a hero and with the fans' adoration for restoring them to the pinnacle of *calcio*. They now blamed De Laurentiis for that glorious period ending so quickly and so unnecessarily.

'It has always been a love–hate relationship and he [De Laurentiis] has often been at the receiving end of abuse from fans for not being from Naples, which is something you can't blame him for,' Kaustubh added. 'That gratefulness from the early years has turned into a considerable amount of bitterness. The amount of banners that criticise him have increased in recent years and there was a point last year when De Laurentiis referred to Naples' citizens as "losers". That didn't go down well with them and the relationship with fans wasn't always perfect even in the title-winning season. A lot of it is usually because of how outspoken De Laurentiis can sometimes be and even though they are quick to swarm him during massive results for the side, that relationship has always been on the edge. The fact that he is regularly at the Maradona gives fans a constant chance to express themselves against him.'

Delivering that precious third Scudetto had not been enough to bring Napoli's fanbase back on to De Laurentiis' side. If anything, it further validated their disappointments and frustrations that their owner could be as destructive as he could be constructive.

Rinascimento is not just the telling of Napoli's triumph. It explores the synergy and shared glory found between two entities yearning for that one shot at a league title. Napoli in their 33-year drought, and Luciano Spalletti's three-decade-long coaching career without a Serie A winners' medal. Spalletti's sensational resignation and return to his Tuscan farm formed the pivot point in his story's latter chapters. Having reached his nirvana of winning a Scudetto in a city that loved and accepted him, it seemed unlikely that he would accept another high-profile move in the near future.

18 August 2023. The Wellington boots had been put away, and the tractor parked in the shed once again. The sabbatical was finished for perhaps the greatest calling of his career. Luciano Spalletti was unveiled as the new head coach of the Italy national team. The reigning European champions had failed to qualify for the 2022 World Cup in Qatar and were experiencing a similarly difficult qualification route to the 2024 European Championship. Roberto Mancini's five-year spell was defined by the Euro 2020 triumph and a record 37-match unbeaten streak. However, the embarrassment of not appearing at the following World Cup proved damaging to his reputation. Tensions with the FIGC were rife following widespread personnel changes behind the scenes, and Mancini resigned ten months before Italy's title defence.

For Spalletti, the tracksuit was swapped for an Emporio Armani suit. This is the Italian national team job, after all. He described the 'indescribable emotion' at being offered the role. 'I feel like a mountaineer who goes to put the flag on Mont Blanc. For me this is the highest task received in my history as a coach.' (*Football Italia*). Three months on, the farm had clearly not affected Spalletti's capacity to engage in press conferences. The task at hand was as treacherous as the Mont Blanc expedition he described in his analogy. Despite being European champions, Italy had lost four of their previous ten matches dating back to mid-2022. That year had been especially cruel to *Gli Azzurri*, mostly for a catastrophic defeat to North Macedonia that denied them World Cup qualification. With the next edition of the European Championship just a year away, Italy had yet to capture the winning aura that had carried them to victory in 2021. Under Roberto Mancini, much of that successful squad had either moved on or suffered significant drops in form, making them a shadow of their previous selves. The likes of Giorgio Chiellini and Leonardo Bonucci fell into the first category, having moved firmly into the autumns of their careers. Leonardo Spinazzola, Manuel Locatelli and Federico Chiesa had all been critical pieces in 2021, but had experienced injury or form issues. Spalletti's job was to not only reinstate that winning feeling, but also progress the squad past the aged core of two years before.

The writing of this book ends before Italy's Championship defence. Their rocky preparations combined with the strength of opposition in the competition might make that a blessing. Without considering the successes or difficulties that Spalletti may encounter, his latest opportunity follows a larger trend that is interwoven across his career in coaching. Unpredictability has marked it at each turn, whether that be close to a decade of difficulty through the 1990s and early 2000s before landing on his feet at Udinese, or storming away from Rome for a prolonged spell in Russia. Becoming national team coach just months after winning his first Serie A title, after which he resigned and vowed to take a sabbatical away from football, was the latest unexpected twist in three decades of intrigue.

Naples will always have 2022/23

FOOTBALL CAN sometimes be over-contextualised. A team's success or failure are deemed so according to factors that are beyond their control. Take Liverpool under Jürgen Klopp as an example. In his near nine years at the club, Klopp won a Premier League title, the Champions League, an FA Cup, the Club World Cup and two League Cups. Looking past the silverware itself, Klopp and Liverpool were such a special marriage because of how he made the fans feel. He bought into the culture of being Liverpudlian and transformed the club in his own image. Few could argue that Klopp was anything but an overwhelming success, a great and even a legend of Liverpool. Yet other factors and variables are used to downplay his achievements. Liverpool could have won two more Premier League titles were it not for being pipped by Pep Guardiola's Manchester City machine. One Champions League triumph could have been three as Liverpool lost two finals to Real Madrid. The context of Liverpool's success is deliberately offset against what they could have won, and not enjoyed for what they did win.

To an extent, this same logic can be applied to Napoli and Luciano Spalletti: the deterioration of any realistic title fight to provide serious competition for them, their own decline in form towards the end of the season, and even the disastrous title defence. Such variables matter when people discuss the greatest-ever sides. However, occasionally it is important to remove context from the debate and just enjoy and appreciate what actually happened. When Klopp waved goodbye to Liverpool in 2024, there was not a dry eye in the house at Anfield that day. Not because they mourned what could have been had they won two more Champions Leagues. They cried because of the joy Klopp had brought to them and the gratitude they felt towards him.

Napoli's dreadful title defence should not cloud the achievement of a year before. Luciano Spalletti's final match in charge did not pull on the heartstrings because Napoli fans were uncertain about the future, or questioned if they would win again. It was because they had been provided with a joyous year that they would remember for the rest of their lives and tell their grandchildren about, and the man who provided that was now leaving.

If you were to provide a counterpoint, you could argue that the mess that followed made Napoli's achievement in 2022/23 even more spectacular. The cracks that emerged had always been there bubbling under the surface and waiting to explode. What Spalletti and that magnificent side did was perform to such a high level that they would not be noticed. After all, Kim Min-jae and Hirving Lozano were the only major casualties between the two seasons. As good as they were in that title-winning team, their loss alone did not spark the collapse of a title winner. Frictions between Aurelio De Laurentiis and the fans, and then between him and the coach, and then between fans and players, were never far away. Spalletti created a team and an identity that elevated itself beyond the noise. Maurizio Sarri had too and were it not for the soul-crushing efficiency of Juventus, that team would have broken the Scudetto curse much sooner than Spalletti's did.

Context matters, but an event as emotionally charged as this requires enjoyment for what is was: a first Serie A title delivered to the city of Naples in over 30 years; the first Serie A title won by Napoli without the aid of Diego Maradona; a style of football that captivated the continent, and at one stage looked like it could challenge for a first-ever Champions League trophy; a team that played thrilling attacking football that combined sophistication and carefully planned patterns with heart and soul and spirit.

Napoli and Naples will always have 2022/23. Those beyond the city walls may one day sneer and point to what followed, but Naples is accustomed to that. The *goduria* of that third Scudetto will endure beyond the lifetimes of those that experienced it. What greater honour can a coach or team bestow than that?

As Luciano Spalletti himself said after the 1-1 draw at Udinese that secured the title: 'Seeing the *Partenopei* smiling and joyful is the greatest emotion for me. They are the ones who pass on their happiness. The problem was reaching this point, as when you have the feelings of an entire city weighing on your back. There are people here who will be able to get through difficult moments in their lives because they remember this moment.'

'These people deserve all the joy.'